THE LUCKY CHANCE

or

THE ALDERMAN'S BARGAIN

APHRA BEHN

Edited by Fidelis Morgan

The Royal Court Writers Series
published by Methuen
in association with the Royal Court Theatre

A METHUEN PAPERBACK

This version of *The Lucky Chance* first published in *The Female Wits* by
Fidelis Morgan, in 1981 by Virago Press Limited
First published in this edition in 1984 by Methuen London Ltd.,
11 New Fetter Lane, London EC4P 4EE
and Methuen Inc, 733 Third Avenue, New York, N.Y. 10017
in association with the Royal Court Theatre, Sloane Square, London SW1.
Copyright © 1981, 1984 by Fidelis Morgan
Introduction copyright © 1984 by Fidelis Morgan
Printed by Expression Printers Ltd, 39 North Road, London N7

Behn, Aphra
    The lucky chance.—(Royal Court writers Series)
    I. Title   II. Morgan Fidelis
    822'.4   PR 3317

    ISBN 0-413-57120-3

Aphra Behn and 'The Lucky Chance'

The Lucky Chance, 'though a very good [play] is too indecent to be ever represented again.' Or so thought the theatre historian John Genest in 1832.

Aphra Behn has always been in trouble for the coarseness of her work. The *Biographic Brittanica*, a late eighteenth century version of the *Dictionary of National Biography*, was not ashamed to include the following article about her:

> The wit of her comedies seems to be generally acknowledged and it is equally acknowledged that they are very indecent, on which account I have not thought myself under any obligation to peruse them. It would have been an unworthy employment nicely to estimate a wit which, having been applied to the purposes of impiety and vice ought not only to be held up in the utmost detestation but consigned if possible to eternal oblivion.

A century later Dr Doran described her in his *Annals of the English Stage*:

> No one equalled this woman in downright nastiness save Ravenscroft and Wycherley . . . With Dryden she vied in indecency, and was not overcome . . . She was a mere harlot who danced through uncleanness and dared them to follow.

When *The Lucky Chance* was first performed at Drury Lane Theatre in April 1686, the criticism Mrs Behn received, mainly from 'wits' and women accusing her of indecency, infuriated her into writing her most eloquent vindication of her right to write.

> And those [critics] I hope will be so kind to me, knowing my conversation not at all addicted to the indecencies alledged, that I would much less practice it in a play that must stand the test of the censoring world. And I must want common sense and all the degrees of good manners, renouncing my fame, all modesty and interest for a silly, saucy, fruitless jest to make fools laugh and women blush and wise men ashamed; myself all the while, if I had been guilty of this crime charged to me, remaining the only stupid, insensible. Is this likely, is this reasonable to be believed by anybody but the wilfully blind? All I ask is the privilege for my masculine part – the poet in me (if any such you will allow me) – to tread in those successful paths my predecessors have so long thrived in, to take those measures that both the ancient and modern writers have set me, and by which they have pleased the world so well. If I must not, because of my sex, have this freedom, but that you will usurp all to yourselves, I lay down my quill, and you shall hear no more of me, no not so much as to make comparisons, because I will be kinder to my brothers of the pen than they have been to a defenceless woman . . . I value fame as much as if I had been born a hero, and if you rob me of that, I can retire from the ungrateful world and scorn its fickle favours.

She did not retire, but continued writing till her death two years later. *The Lucky Chance* remained a stock piece in the London repertoire for the following decade.

Virginia Woolf suggested that 'all women together ought to let flowers fall upon the tomb of Aphra Behn . . . for it was she who earned them the right to speak their minds.' Unfortunately the position of Aphra Behn's tomb is one of the few certain facts of her life. She is buried in Westminster Abbey under a black marble slab bearing the couplet:

Here lies a proof that wit can never be
Defence enough against mortality.

She was, after Dryden, the most prolific writer of the age, and she left eighteen plays and many novels, prose works, poems and translations as a more appropriate monument.

She was the first woman to write for a living, driven by debts run up while spying for the English government in the Dutch Wars.

She seems, during her youth, to have visited Surinam in South America, and returned with some rare flies which she presented to His Majesty's Antiquaries (the seventeenth century's Natural History collection) and an Indian costume made from beautifully coloured feathers and wreaths which she gave to the King's Theatre.

She had an unfortunate long-term relationship with a lawyer, John Hoyle, known to be 'an atheist, a sodomite professed, a corrupter of youth and a blasphemer of Christ'. This black-eyed beau was brought before a grand jury at the Old Bailey on a charge of sodomy with a poulterer shortly before Aphra Behn's death, and discharged with a not-proven verdict.

Most of the other information about Mrs Behn derives from apocryphal tales from the seventeenth century or vivid imaginations in the centuries since.

One of the rather dubious claims is that she introduced the beverage milk punch into England.

In her first play, *The Forced Marriage*, a young man called Thomas Otway made his first and last appearance as an actor. The sight of a full house on the first night put him into such a sweat that he did not even make it to the second. Although he had no future *on* stage his contribution to the theatre was a handful of strong plays, including the frequently performed tragedy, *Venice Preserved*. Otway died in poverty in 1685. He was 34. A spurious tale suggests that he choked to death on a crust of bread, his first food for days.

The Lucky Chance was ready for production in the following spring. The character of Gayman in this play bears more than a passing resemblance to the character and circumstances of the unfortunate Otway, and can be seen as Aphra Behn's tribute to him. Thomas Betterton took the role of Gayman, and Lady Fulbank, Gayman's witty and forceful mistress, was played by Elizabeth Barry, with whom Otway had been infatuated for many years.

The two leading comic actors Anthony Leigh and James Nokes took the parts of Sir Feeble and Sir Cautious.

It seems that *The Lucky Chance* has not been seen on the London stage since 1718.

Fidelis Morgan

Characters

BELLMOUR, *in love with Leticia, in hiding to avoid arrest for his part in a duel*

LETICIA, *young and virginal, but about to marry Sir Feeble Fainwood*

GAYMAN, *a spark of the town, in love with Julia but impoverished and going under the name of Wasteall*

JULIA, *now* LADY FULBANK, *honest and generous, in love with Gayman, but recently married to a wealthy banker, Sir Cautious Fulbank*

SIR FEEBLE FAINWOOD, *an old alderman, about to be married to Leticia*

SIR CAUTIOUS FULBANK, *an old banker, already married to Julia*

DIANA, *daughter to Sir Feeble Fainwood, virtuous and in love with Bredwell*

BREDWELL, *brother to Leticia and apprenticed to Sir Cautious Fulbank, in love with Diana*

BEARJEST, *a nephew to Sir Cautious Fulbank, a fop, wooing Diana*

CAPTAIN NOISEY, *Bearjest's friend and companion*

GAMMER GRIME, *a blacksmith's wife and Gayman's landlady*

PERT, *maidservant to Julia*

PHILLIS, *maidservant to Leticia*

SUSAN, *maidservant to Sir Feeble Fainwood*

RAG, *footman to Gayman*

RALPH, *footman to Sir Feeble*

DICK, *footman to Sir Cautious*

MR CHEEK, *a musician*

MR GINGLE, *a musician*

A parson, a shepherd, fiddlers, dancers, singers, porters, servants, postman

The action takes place in London.

The Lucky Chance was first performed at the Drury Lane Theatre *c.* April 1686. After more than 250 years of neglect, it was presented by the Women's Playhouse Trust, as its inaugural production, at the Royal Court Theatre, London, on 4 July, with the following cast:

BELLMOUR	Denis Lawson
LETICIA	Katherine Pogson
GAYMAN	Alan Rickman
JULIA	Harriet Walter
SIR FEEBLE FAINWOOD	Jonathan Adam
SIR CAUTIOUS FULBANK	Paul Bacon
DIANA	Francesca Brill
BREDWELL	Mark Tandy
BEARJEST	Christopher Fairbank
All other parts played by	Pam Ferris

Directed by Jules Wright
Designed by Jenny Tiramani
Lighting by Geoffrey Joyce
Music by Ilona Sekacz
Choreography by Jacky Lansley

Note: The use of square brackets in the text indicates cuts made for the WPT production.

ACT I

THE STREET, AT BREAK OF DAY

Enter BELLMOUR, *disguised in a travelling habit*

BELLMOUR   Sure 'tis the day that gleams in yonder east,
The day that all but lovers blest by shade
Pay cheerful homage to:
Lovers, and those pursued like guilty me
By rigid laws, which put no difference
'Twixt fairly killing in my own defence,
And murders bred by drunken arguments,
Whores, or the mean revenges of a coward.
This is Leticia's father's house. . . (*Looking about*)
And that the dear balcony
That has so oft been conscious of our loves;
From whence she's sent me down a thousand sighs,
A thousand looks of love, a thousand vows!
O thou dear witness of those charming hours,
How do I bless thee, how am I pleased to view thee
After a tedious age of six months' banishment.

Enter several musicians

FIDDLER   But hark ye, Mr Gingle, is it proper to play before the
wedding?
GINGLE   Ever while you live, for many a time in playing after the
first night, the bride's sleepy, the bridegroom tired, and both so out
of humour, that perhaps they hate anything that puts 'em in mind
they are married.

They play and sing

> [*Rise, Cloris, charming maid arise!*
> *And baffle breaking day,*
> *Show the adoring world thy eyes*
> *Are more surprising gay;*
> *The Gods of love are smiling round,*
> *And lead the bridegroom on,*
> *And Hymen has the altar crowned,*
> *While all thy sighing lovers are undone.*
>
> *To see thee pass they throng the plain;*
> *The groves with flowers are strown,*
> *And every young and envying swain*

Wishes the hour his own.
Rise then, and let the God of day,
When thou dost to the lover yield,
Behold more treasure given away
Than he in his vast circle e'er beheld.]

Enter PHILLIS *on the balcony; throws them money*

BELLMOUR   Hah, Phillis, Leticia's woman!
GINGLE   Fie, Mrs Phillis, do you take us for fiddlers that play for
hire? I came to compliment Mrs Leticia on her wedding morning
because she is my scholar.
PHILLIS   She sends it only to drink her health.
GINGLE   Come, lads, let's to the tavern then.

Exeunt musicians

BELLMOUR   Hah! Said he Leticia?
Sure I shall turn to marble at this news,
I harden, and cold damps pass through my senseless pores.
Ha, who's here?

Enter GAYMAN, *wrapped in his cloak*

GAYMAN   'Tis yet too early, but my soul's impatient.
And I must see Leticia. (*Goes to the door*)
BELLMOUR   Death and the devil, the bridegroom!
Stay, Sir, by heaven you pass not this way.

Goes to the door as he is knocking, pushes him away, and draws

GAYMAN   Hah! What art thou that durst forbid me entrance? Stand
off.

They fight a little, and closing view each other

BELLMOUR   Gayman!
GAYMAN   My dearest Bellmour!
BELLMOUR   Oh thou false friend, thou treacherous base deceiver!
GAYMAN   Hah, this to me, dear Harry?
BELLMOUR   Whither is honour, truth and friendship fled?
GAYMAN   Why, there ne'er was such a virtue, 'Tis all a poet's
dream.
BELLMOUR   I thank you, Sir.
GAYMAN   I'm sorry for't, or that ever I did anything that could
deserve it: put up your sword, an honest man would say how he's
offended, before he rashly draws.
BELLMOUR   Are you not going to be married, Sir?
GAYMAN   No Sir, not as long as any man in London is so, that has
but a handsome wife, Sir.

BELLMOUR   Are not you in love, Sir?

GAYMAN   Most damnably, and would fain lie with the dear jilting gipsy.

BELLMOUR   Hah, who would you lie with, Sir?

GAYMAN   You catechise me roundly, 'tis not fair to name, but I am no starter, Harry, just as you left me, you find me. I am for the faithless Julia still, the old Alderman's wife. 'Twas high time the city should lose their charter, when their wives turn honest. But pray, Sir, answer me a question or two.

BELLMOUR   Answer me first, what make you here this morning?

GAYMAN   Faith, to do you service. Your damned little jade of a mistress has learned of her neighbours the art of swearing and lying in abundance, and is—

BELLMOUR (*Sighing*)   To be married!

GAYMAN   Even so, God save the mark, and she'll be a fair one for many an arrow besides her husband's, though he's an old Finsbury hero this threescore years.

BELLMOUR   Who mean you?

GAYMAN   Why, thy cuckold that shall be, if thou be'st wise.

BELLMOUR   Away! Who is this man? Thou dalliest with me.

GAYMAN   Why, an old knight, and alderman here o' th' city, Sir Feeble Fainwood, a jolly old fellow, whose activity is all got into his tongue, a very excellent teaser, but neither youth nor beauty can grind his dudgeon to an edge.

BELLMOUR   Fie, what stuff's here!

GAYMAN   Very excellent stuff, if you have but the grace to improve it.

BELLMOUR   You banter me, but in plain English tell me, what made you here thus early, entering yon house with such authority?

GAYMAN   Why, your mistress Leticia, your contracted wife, is this morning to be married to old Sir Feeble Fainwood, induced to't I suppose by the great jointure he makes her, and the improbability of your ever gaining your pardon for your high duel. Do I speak English now, Sir?

BELLMOUR   Too well; would I had never heard thee.

GAYMAN   Now I being the confidant in your amours, the Jack-go-between, the civil pimp, or so, you left her in charge with me at your departure.

BELLMOUR   I did so.

GAYMAN   I saw her every day, and every day she paid the tribute of a shower of tears, to the dear lord of all her vows, young Bellmour. Till, faith, at last, for reasons manifold I slacked my daily visits.

BELLMOUR   And left her to temptation, was that well done?

GAYMAN   Now must I afflict you and myself with a long tale of causes why, or be charged with want of friendship.

BELLMOUR   You will do well to clear that point with me.

GAYMAN   I see you're peevish, and you shall be humoured. You
know my Julia played me e'en such another prank as your false one
is going to play you, and married old Sir Cautious Fulbank here
i'th' city; at which you know I stormed, and raved, and swore, as
thou would now, and to as little purpose. There was but one way
left, and that was cuckolding him.

BELLMOUR   Well, that design I left thee hot upon.

GAYMAN   And hotly have pursued it: swore, wept, vowed, wrote,
upbraided, prayed and railed, then treated lavishly, and presented
high, till, between you and I, Harry, I have presented the best part
of eight hundred a year into her husband's hands, in mortgage.

BELLMOUR   This is the course you'd have me steer, I thank you.

GAYMAN   No, no, pox on't, all women are not jilts. Some are honest,
and will give as well as take, or else there would not be so many broke
i'th' city. In fine, Sir, I have been in tribulation, that is to say,
moneyless, for six tedious weeks, without either clothes, or equipage
to appear withal, and so not only my own love affair lay neglected,
but thine too, and I am forced to pretend to my lady that I am
i'th' country with a dying uncle, from whom, if he were indeed dead,
I expect two thousand a year.

BELLMOUR   But what's all this to being here this morning?

GAYMAN   Thus have I lain concealed like a winter fly, hoping for
some blessed sunshine to warm me into life again, and make me
hover my flagging wings, till the news of this marriage (which fills
the town) made me crawl out this silent hour, to upbraid the fickle
maid.

BELLMOUR   Did'st thou? Pursue thy kind design. Get me to see her,
and sure no woman, even possessed with a new passion, grown
confident even to prostitution, but when she sees the man to whom
she's sworn so very very much, will find remorse and shame.

GAYMAN   For your sake, though the day be broke upon us, and I'm
undone, if seen, I'll venture in. . . (*Throws his cloak over*)

Enter SIR FEEBLE FAINWOOD, SIR CAUTIOUS FULBANK,
BEARJEST, *and* NOISEY. *They pass over the stage, and go into the
house*

Hah, see the bridegroom! And with him my destined cuckold, old
Sir Cautious Fulbank. Hah, what ail'st thou, man?

BELLMOUR   The bridegroom! Like Gorgon's head he's turned me
into stone.

GAYMAN   Gorgon's head, a cuckold's head, 'twas made to graft upon.

BELLMOUR   By heaven I'll seize her even at the altar, and bear her
thence in triumph.

GAYMAN   Ay, and be borne to Newgate in triumph, and be hanged in triumph. 'Twil! be cold comfort, celebrating your nuptials in the press-yard, and be waked next morning, like Mr Barnardine in the play. Will you please to rise and be hanged a little, Sir?

BELLMOUR   What wouldst thou have me to do?

GAYMAN   As many an honest man has done before thee. . . cuckold him, cuckold him.

BELLMOUR   What, and let him marry her! She that's mine by sacred vow already! By heaven it would be flat adultery in her!

GAYMAN   She'll learn the trick, and practise it the better with thee.

BELLMOUR   O heavens! Leticia marry him and lie with him! Here will I stand and see this shameful woman, see if she dares pass by me to this wickedness.

GAYMAN   Hark ye, Harry, in earnest have a care of betraying yourself; and do not venture sweet life for a fickle woman, who perhaps hates you.

BELLMOUR   You counsel well, but to see her married! How every thought of that shocks all my resolution! But hang it, I'll be resolute and saucy, despise a woman who can use me ill, and think myself above her.

GAYMAN   Why, now thou art thyself, a man again. But see, they're coming forth, now stand your ground.

Enter SIR FEEBLE, SIR CAUTIOUS, BEARJEST, NOISEY, LETICIA, *sad,* DIANA, PHILLIS. *They pass over the stage*

BELLMOUR   'Tis she! Support me, Charles, or I shall sink to earth. Methought in passing by she cast a scornful glance at me. Such charming pride I've seen upon her eyes, when our love quarrels armed 'em with disdain. I'll after 'em; if I live she shall not 'scape me.

BELLMOUR *offers to go,* GAYMAN *holds him*

GAYMAN   Hold, remember you're proscribed, and die if you are taken.

BELLMOUR   I've done, and I will live, but he shall ne'er enjoy her. Who's yonder? Ralph, my trusty confidant?

Enter RÀLPH

Now though I perish I must speak to him. Friend, what wedding's this?

RALPH   One that was never made in heaven, Sir; 'tis Alderman Fainwood, and Mrs Leticia Bredwell.

BELLMOUR   Bredwell, I have heard of her, she was mistress—

RALPH   To fine Mr Bellmour, Sir, ay, there was a gentleman. . . But rest his soul, he's hanged, Sir. (*Weeps*)

BELLMOUR   How! Hanged?

RALPH   Hanged, Sir, hanged, at The Hague in Holland.

GAYMAN   I heard some such news, but did not credit it.

BELLMOUR   For what, said they, was he hanged?

RALPH   Why, e'en for high treason, Sir, he killed one of their kings.

GAYMAN   Holland's a commonwealth, and is not ruled by kings.

RALPH   Not by one, Sir, but by many. This was a cheesemonger, they fell out over a bottle of brandy, went to snicker snee, Mr Bellmour cut his throat, and was hanged for't, that's all, Sir.

BELLMOUR   And did the young lady believe this?

RALPH   Yes, and took on most heavily, the doctors gave her over, and there was the devil to do to get her to consent to this marriage. But her fortune was small, and the hope of a ladyship, and a gold chain at the Spittal sermon, did the business, and so your servant, Sir.

Exit RALPH

BELLMOUR   So, here's a hopeful account of my sweet self now.

Enter POSTMAN *with letters*

POSTMAN   Pray, Sir, which is Sir Feeble Fainwood's?

BELLMOUR   What would you with him, friend?

POSTMAN   I have a letter here from The Hague for him.

BELLMOUR   (From The Hague! Now have I a curiosity to see it.) I am his servant, give it me. (POSTMAN *gives it him, and exits*) Perhaps here may be the second part of my tragedy. I'm full of mischief, Charles, and have a mind to see this fellow's secrets. For from this hour I'll be his evil genius, haunt him at bed and board, he shall not sleep nor eat, disturb him at his prayers, in his embraces, and tease him into madness. Help me, invention, malice, love and wit. (*Opening the letter*) Ye Gods, and little fiends, instruct my mischief. (*Reads*)

'Dear Brother,
According to your desire I have sent for my son from St Omer's, whom I have sent to wait on you in England. He is a very good accountant, and fit for business, and much pleased he shall see that Uncle to whom he's so obliged, and which is so gratefully acknowledged by, dear brother,
Your affectionate brother,

Francis Fainwood'

Hum, hark ye, Charles, do you know who I am now?

GAYMAN   Why, I hope a very honest friend of mine, Harry Bellmour.

BELLMOUR   No, Sir, you are mistaken in your man.

GAYMAN   It may be so.

BELLMOUR   I am, d'ye see, Charles, this very individual, numerical young Mr . . . what ye call 'um Fainwood, just come from St Omer's into England, to my Uncle the Alderman. I am, Charles, this very man.

GAYMAN   I know you are, and will swear't upon occasion.

BELLMOUR   This lucky thought has almost calmed my mind. And if I don't fit you, my dear Uncle, may I never lie with my Aunt.

GAYMAN   Ah, rogue, but prithee what care have you taken about your pardon? 'Twere good you should secure that.

BELLMOUR   There's the devil, Charles, had I but that. . . but that seldom fails, but yet in vain, I being the first transgressor since the Act against duelling. But I am impatient to see this dear delight of my soul, and hearing from none of you this six weeks, came from Brussels in this disguise, for the Hague I have not seen, though hanged there. But come, let's away, and complete me a right St Omer's spark, that I may present myself as soon as they come from church.

SCENE II

INSIDE SIR CAUTIOUS FULBANK'S HOUSE

Enter LADY FULBANK, PERT *and* BREDWELL. BREDWELL *gives her a letter*

LADY FULBANK (*reads*)   'Did my Julia know how I languish in this cruel separation, she would afford me her pity, and write oftener. If only the expectation of two thousand a year kept me from you, ah, Julia, how easily would I abandon that trifle for your more valued sight; but that I know a fortune will render me more agreeable to the charming Julia, I should quit all my interest here, to throw myself at her feet, to make her sensible how I am entirely her adorer, Charles Gayman.' Faith, Charles you lie, you are as welcome to me now, now when I doubt thy fortune is declining, as if the universe were thine.

PERT   That, Madam, is a noble gratitude. For if his fortune be declining, 'tis sacrificed to his passion for your ladyship. 'Tis all laid out on love.

LADY FULBANK   I prize my honour more than life. Yet I had rather have given him all he wished of me, than be guilty of his undoing.

PERT   And I think the sin were less.

LADY FULBANK   I must confess, such jewels, rings and presents as he made me must needs decay his fortune.

BREDWELL   Ay, Madam, his very coach at last was turned into a jewel for your ladyship. Then, Madam, what expenses his despair have run him on. . . as drinking and gaming, to divert the thought of your marrying my old master.

LADY FULBANK   And put in wenching, too.

BREDWELL   No, assure yourself, Madam.

LADY FULBANK (*to* BREDWELL)   Of that I would be better satisfied, and you too must assist me, as e'er you hope I should be kind to you in gaining you Diana.

BREDWELL   Madam, I'll die to serve you.

PERT   Nor will I be behind in my duty.

LADY FULBANK   Oh, how fatal are forced marriages!
How many ruins one such match pulls on!
Had I but kept my sacred vows to Gayman,
How happy had I been, how prosperous he!
Whilst now I languish in a loathed embrace,
Pine out my life with age, consumptions, coughs.
But dost thou fear that Gayman is declining?

BREDWELL   You are my lady, and the best of mistresses, therefore I would not grieve you, for I know you love this best, but most unhappy man.

LADY FULBANK   You shall not grieve me, prithee on.

BREDWELL   My master sent me yesterday to Mr Crap his scrivener, to send to one Mr Wasteall, to tell him his first mortgage was out, which is two hundred pounds a year, and who has since engaged five or six hundred more to my master. But if this first be not redeemed, he'll take the forfeit on't, as he says a wise man ought.

LADY FULBANK   That is to say, a knave, according to his notion of a wise man.

BREDWELL   Mr Crap, being busy with a borrowing Lord, sent me to Mr Wasteall, whose lodging is in a nasty place called Alsatia, at a black-smith's.

LADY FULBANK   But what's all this to Gayman?

BREDWELL   Madam, this Wasteall was Mr Gayman.

LADY FULBANK   Gayman! Saw'st thou Gayman?

BREDWELL   Madam, Mr Gayman, yesterday.

LADY FULBANK   When came he to town?

BREDWELL   Madam, he has not been out of it.

LADY FULBANK   Not at his Uncle's in Northamptonshire?

BREDWELL   Your ladyship was wont to credit me.

LADY FULBANK   Forgive me, you went to a blacksmith's.

BREDWELL   Yes Madam, and at the door encountered the beastly thing he calls a landlady, who looked as if she had been of her own husband's making, composed of moulded smith's dust. I asked for Mr Wasteall, and she began to open, and did so rail at him, that what with her Billingsgate, and her husband's hammers, I was both deaf and dumb. At last the hammers ceased, and she grew weary, and called down Mr Wasteall. But he not answering I was sent up a ladder rather than a pair of stairs. At last I scaled the top, and entered the enchanted castle; there did I find him, spite of the noise below, drowning his cares in sleep.

LADY FULBANK   Whom found'st thou? Gayman?

BREDWELL   He, Madam, whom I waked, and seeing me, Heavens what confusion seized him, which nothing but my own surprise could equal. Ashamed, he would have turned away, but when he saw, by my dejected eyes, I knew him, he sighed, and blushed, and heard me tell my business. Then begged I would be secret, for he vowed his whole repose and life depended on my silence. Nor had I told it now, but that your Ladyship may find some speedy means to draw him from this desperate condition.

LADY FULBANK   Heavens, is't possible?

BREDWELL   He's driven to the last degree of poverty. Had you but seen his lodgings, Madam!

LADY FULBANK   What were they?

BREDWELL   'Tis a pretty convenient tub, Madam. He may lie along in't. There's just room for an old joined stool besides the bed, which one cannot call a cabin, about the largeness of a pantry bin, or a usurer's trunk. There had been dornex curtains to't in the days of yore, but they were now annihilated, and nothing left to save his eyes from the light but my landlady's blue apron, tied by the strings before the window, in which stood a broken six-penny looking-glass, that showed as many faces as the scene in Henry the Eighth, which could but just stand upright, and then the comb case filled it.

LADY FULBANK   What a lewd description hast thou made of his chamber.

BREDWELL   Then for his equipage, 'tis banished to one small Monsieur, who, saucy with his master's poverty, is rather a companion than a footman.

LADY FULBANK   But what said he to the forfeiture of his land?

BREDWELL   He sighed and cried, 'Why, farewell dirty acres; It shall not trouble me, since 'twas all for love!'

LADY FULBANK   How much redeems it?

BREDWELL   Madam, five hundred pounds.

LADY FULBANK   Enough, you shall in some disguise convey this money to him, as from an unknown hand, I would not have him think it comes from me, for all the world. That nicety and virtue I protest I am resolved to keep.

PERT   If I were your ladyship, I would make use of Sir Cautious's cash: pay him in his own coin.

BREDWELL   Your Ladyship would make no scruple of it, if you knew how this poor gentleman has been used by my unmerciful master.

LADY FULBANK   I have a key already to his counting house; it being lost, he had another made, and this I found and kept.

BREDWELL   Madam, this is an excellent time for't, my master being gone to give my sister Leticia at church.

LADY FULBANK   'Tis so, and I'll go and commit the theft, whilst you prepare to carry it, and then we'll to dinner with your sister, the bride.

SCENE III

THE HOUSE OF SIR FEEBLE

Enter SIR FEEBLE, LETICIA, SIR CAUTIOUS, BEARJEST, DIANA, *and* NOISEY. SIR FEEBLE *sings and salutes them*

SIR FEEBLE   Welcome! *Joan Sanderson*! Welcome, welcome. (*Kisses the bride*) Ods bobs, and so thou art, sweetheart.

BEARJEST   Methinks my lady bride is very melancholy.

SIR CAUTIOUS   Ay, ay, women that are discreet are always thus upon their wedding day.

SIR FEEBLE   Always by day-light, Sir Cautious. (*Sings*)

> *But when bright Phoebus does retire,*
> *To Thetis' bed to quench his fire,*
> *And do the thing we need not name,*
> *We mortals by his influence do the same.*
> *Then, then the blushing maid lays by*
> *Her simpering, and her modesty;*
> *And round the lover clasps and twines*
> *Like ivy, or the circling vines.*

Here, Ralph, the bottle, rogue, of sack, ye rascal. Hadst thou been a butler worth hanging thou wouldst have met us at the door with it. Ods bobs, sweetheart, thy health.

BEARJEST   Away with it, to the bride's Haunce in Kelder.

SIR FEEBLE   Go to, go to, rogue, go to, that shall be, knave, that shall be the morrow morning. He, ods bobs, we'll do't, sweetheart; here's to't. (*Drinks again*)

LETICIA   I die but to imagine it, would I were dead indeed.

SIR FEEBLE   Hah, hum, how's this? Tears upon the wedding day? Why, why, you baggage you, ye little ting, fool's face, away you rogue, you're naughty, you're naughty. (*Patting and playing, and following her*) Look, look, look now, buss it, buss it, buss it and friends; did'ums, did'ums beat its none silly baby, away you little hussy, away, and pledge me. . .

She drinks a little

SIR CAUTIOUS   A wise discreet lady, I'll warrant her. My lady would prodigally have took it off all.

SIR FEEBLE   Dears, its nown dear Fubs, buss again, buss again, away, away, away, ods bobs, I long for night, look, look Sir Cautious, what an eye's there!

SIR CAUTIOUS   Ay, so there is, brother, and a modest eye too.

SIR FEEBLE   Adad, I love her more and more. Ralph, call old Susan hither. Come Mr Bearjest, put the glass about. Ods bobs, when I was a young fellow I would not let the young wenches look pale and wan, but would rouse 'em and touse 'em, and blowze 'em, till I put a colour in their cheeks, like an apple John, assacks. Nay, I can make a shift still, and pupsey shall not be jealous.

Enter SUSAN. SIR FEEBLE *whispers to her, she goes out*

LETICIA   Indeed not I, Sir, I shall be all obedience.

SIR CAUTIOUS   A most judicious lady, would my Julia had a little of her modesty. But my lady's a wit.

Re-enter SUSAN, *with a box*

SIR FEEBLE   Look here my little puskin, here's fine play-things for its nown little coxcomb, go, get you gone, get you gone, and off with these St Martin's trumpery, these play-house glass baubles, this necklace, and these pendants, and all this false ware; ods bobs, I'll have no counterfeit gear about thee, not I. See these are right as the blushes on thy cheeks, and these as true as my heart, girl. Go, put 'em on, and be fine. (*Gives them to her*)

LETICIA   Believe me, Sir, I shall not merit this kindness.

SIR FEEBLE   Go to, more of your love, and less of your ceremony, give the old fool a hearty buss, and pay him that way. Hark ye, little wanton tit, I'll steal up and catch ye and love ye, adod I will. Get ye gone, get ye gone.

LETICIA   Heavens, what a nauseous thing is an old man turned lover!

Exeunt LETICIA *and* DIANA

SIR CAUTIOUS   How, steal up, Sir Feeble? I hope not so. I hold it most indecent before the lawful hour.

SIR FEEBLE   Lawful hour! Why, I hope all hours are lawful with a man's own wife.

SIR CAUTIOUS   But wise men have respect to times and seasons.

SIR FEEBLE   Wise young men, Sir Cautious; but wise old men must nick their inclinations, for it is not as 'twas wont to be, for it is not as 'twas wont to be. (*Singing and dancing*)

Enter RALPH

RALPH   Sir, here's a young gentleman without would speak with you.
SIR FEEBLE   Hum, I hope it is not that same Bellmour come to forbid the banns; if it be, he comes too late, therefore bring me first my long sword, and then the gentleman.

Exit RALPH

BEARJEST   Pray Sir, use mine, it is a travelled blade I can assure you, Sir.
SIR FEEBLE   I thank you, Sir.

Enter RALPH *and* BELLMOUR *disguised, gives* SIR FEEBLE *a letter. He reads*

How. . . my nephew! Francis Fainwood! (*Embraces him*)
BELLMOUR   (I am glad he has told me my christian name.)
SIR FEEBLE   Sir Cautious, know my nephew, 'tis a young St Omer's scholar, but none of the witnesses.
SIR CAUTIOUS   Marry, Sir, and the wiser he, for they got nothing by't.
BEARJEST   Sir, I love and honour you, because you are a traveller.
SIR FEEBLE   A very proper young fellow, and as like old Frank Fainwood as the devil to the collier. But, Francis, you are come into a very lewd town, Francis, for whoring, and plotting, and roaring, and drinking, but you must go to church, Francis, and avoid ill company, or you may make damnable havoc in my cash, Francis, what! You can keep merchants' books?
BELLMOUR   That's been my study, Sir.
SIR FEEBLE   And you will not be proud, but will be commanded by me, Francis?
BELLMOUR   I desire not to be favoured as a kinsman, Sir, but as your humblest servant.
SIR FEEBLE   Why, thou'rt an honest fellow, Francis, and thou'rt heartily welcome, and I'll make thee fortunate. But come, Sir Cautious, let you and I take a turn i'th' garden, and get a right understanding between your nephew Mr Bearjest, and my daughter Dy.
SIR CAUTIOUS   Prudently thought on, Sir, I'll wait on you.

Exeunt SIR FEEBLE, *and* SIR CAUTIOUS

BEARJEST   You are a traveller, I understand.
BELLMOUR   I have seen a little part of the whole world, Sir.
BEARJEST   So have I, Sir, I thank my stars, and have performed most of my travels on foot, Sir.
BELLMOUR   You did not travel far then, I presume, Sir?

BEARJEST   No, Sir, it was for my diversion indeed, but I assure you, I travelled into Ireland a-foot, Sir.

BELLMOUR   Sure, Sir, you go by shipping into Ireland?

BEARJEST   That's all one, Sir, I was still a-foot, ever walking on the deck.

BELLMOUR   Was that your farthest travel, Sir?

BEARJEST   Farthest, why that's the end of the world, and sure a man can go no farther.

BELLMOUR   Sure, there can be nothing worth a man's curiosity?

BEARJEST   No, Sir, I'll assure you, there are the wonders of the world. Sir, I'll hint you this one. There is a harbour which since the creation was never capable of receiving a lighter, yet by another miracle the King of France was to ride there with a vast fleet of ships, and to land a hundred thousand men.

BELLMOUR   This is a swinging wonder, but are there store of madmen there, Sir?

BEARJEST   That's another rarity, to see a man run out of his wits.

NOISEY   Marry, Sir, the wiser they, I say.

BEARJEST   Pray Sir, what store of miracles have you at St Omer's?

BELLMOUR   None, Sir, since that of the wonderful Salamanca doctor, who was both here and there at the same instant of time.

BEARJEST   How, Sir? Why, that's impossible.

BELLMOUR   That was the wonder, Sir, because 'twas impossible.

NOISEY   But 'twas a greater, Sir, that 'twas believed.

Enter LADY FULBANK, PERT, SIR CAUTIOUS, *and* SIR FEEBLE

SIR FEEBLE   Enough, enough, Sir Cautious, we apprehend one another. Mr Bearjest, your uncle here and I have struck the bargain, the wench is yours with three thousand pound present, and something more after death, which your uncle likes well.

BEARJEST   Does he so, Sir, I'm beholden to him. Then 'tis not a pin matter whether I like or not, Sir.

SIR FEEBLE   How, Sir, not like my daughter Dy?

BEARJEST   Oh Lord, Sir, die or live, 'tis all one for that, Sir, I'll stand to the bargain my uncle makes.

PERT   Will you so, Sir? You'll have very good luck if you do.

BEARJEST   Prithee, hold thy peace, my lady's woman.

LADY FULBANK   Sir, I beg your pardon for not waiting on you to church, I knew you would be private.

Enter LETICIA, *in fine jewels*

SIR FEEBLE   You honour us too highly now, Madam.

SIR FEEBLE *presents his wife, who salutes her*

LADY FULBANK   Give you joy, my dear Leticia! I find, Sir, you were
    resolved for youth, wit and beauty.
SIR FEEBLE   Ay, ay, Madam, to the comfort of many a hoping
    coxcomb. But Lette, rogue Lette, thou would not make me free o'th'
    city a second time. Would thou entice the rogues with the twire and
    the wanton leer, the amorous simper that cries 'come kiss me', then
    the pretty round lips are pouted out? The rogue, how I long to be at
    'em! Well, she shall never go to church more, that she shall not.
LADY FULBANK   How, Sir, not to church, the chiefest recreation of
    a city lady?
SIR FEEBLE   That's all one, Madam, that tricking and dressing, and
    prinking and patching is not your devotion to heaven, but to the
    young knaves that are licked and combed and are minding you more
    than the parson. Ods bobs, there are more cuckolds destined in the
    church, than are made out of it.
SIR CAUTIOUS   Ha, ha, ha, he tickles ye i'faith, ladies.
BELLMOUR   Not one chance look this way, and yet,
    I can forgive her lovely eyes,
    Because they look not pleased with all this ceremony,
    And yet, methinks, some sympathy in love
    Might this way glance their beams. . . I cannot hold
    . . . Sir, is this fair lady my aunt?
SIR FEEBLE   Oh Francis! Come hither, Francis. Lette, here's a young
    rogue has a mind to kiss thee.

    SIR FEEBLE *puts them together, she starts back*

    Nay, start not, he's my own flesh and blood, my nephew, baby. Look,
    look how the young rogues stare at one another; like will to like, I
    see that.
LETICIA   There's something in his face so like my Bellmour, it calls
    my blushes up, and leaves my heart defenceless.

    Enter RALPH

RALPH   Sir, dinner's on the table.
SIR FEEBLE   Come, come, let's in then, gentlemen and ladies,
    And share today my pleasures and delight,
    But. . .
    Adds bobs, they must be all mine own at night.

ACT II

SCENE I

GAYMAN'S LODGINGS

Enter GAYMAN *in a night-cap, and an old campaign coat tied about him, very melancholy*

GAYMAN   Curse on my birth! Curse on my faithless fortune!
Curse on my stars, and curst be all, but love!
That dear, that charming sin, though 't have pulled
Innumerable mischiefs on my head,
I have not, nor I cannot find repentance for.
No, let me die despised, upbraided, poor:
Let fortune, friends and all abandon me
But let me hold thee, thou soft smiling God,
Close to my heart while life continues there.
Till the last panting of my vital blood,
Nay, the last spark of life and fire be love's!

Enter RAG

How now, Rag, what's o'clock?
RAG   My belly can inform you better than my tongue.
GAYMAN   Why, you gormandizing vermin you, what have you done
with the three pence I gave you a fortnight ago?
RAG   Alas, Sir, that's all gone long since.
GAYMAN   You gutling rascal, you are enough to breed a famine in a
land. I have known some industrious footmen that have not only
gotten their own living, but a pretty livelihood for their masters, too.
RAG   Ay, till they came to the gallows, Sir.
GAYMAN   Very well, Sirrah, they died in an honourable calling, but
hark ye, Rag, I have business, very earnest business abroad this
evening. Now, were you a rascal of docity, you would invent a way
to get home my last suit that was laid in lavender, with the appurtenances
thereunto belonging, as periwig, cravat, and so forth.
RAG   Faith, master, I must deal in the black art then, for no human
means will do't. And now I talk of the black art, Master, try your
power once more with my landlady.
GAYMAN   Oh! name her not, the thought on't turns my stomach, a
sight of her is a vomit; but he's a bold hero that dares venture on her
for a kiss, and all beyond that sure is hell itself, yet there's my last,
last refuge, and I must to this wedding. I know not what, but
something whispers me, this night I shall be happy, and without
Julia 'tis impossible!

RAG   Julia, who's that? my Lady Fulbank, Sir?

GAYMAN   Peace, Sirrah, and call. . . a. . . no, pox on't, come back. . . and yet. . . yes. . . call my fulsome landlady.

Exit RAG

Sir Cautious knows me not by name or person. And I will to this wedding, I'm sure of seeing Julia there, and what may come of that. But here's old Nasty coming, I smell her up. Hah, my dear landlady.

Enter RAG *and* LANDLADY

Quite out of breath, a chair there for my landlady.

RAG   Here's ne'er a one, Sir.

LANDLADY   More of your money and less of your civility, good Mr Wasteall.

GAYMAN   Dear landlady. . .

LANDLADY   Dear me no dears, Sir, but let me have my money, eight weeks' rent last Friday; besides taverns, ale-houses, chandlers, laundresses' scores, and ready money out of my purse, you know it, Si

GAYMAN   Ay, but your husband don't. Speak softly.

LANDLADY   My husband! What, do you think to fright me with my husband? I'd have you to know I'm an honest woman, and care not this. . . for my husband. Is this all the thanks I have for my kindness, for patching, borrowing and shifting for you? 'Twas but last week I pawned my best petticoat, as I hope to wear it again, it cost me six and twenty shillings besides making, then this morning my new Norwich mantua followed, and two postle spoons, I had the whole dozen when you came first, but they dropped, and dropped, till I had only Judas left for my husband.

GAYMAN   Hear me, good landlady.

LANDLADY   Then I've passed my word at the George Tavern for forty shillings for you, ten shillings at my neighbour Squabs for ale, besides seven shillings to mother Suds for washing, and do you fob me off with my husband?

GAYMAN   Here, Rag, run and fetch her a pint of sack, there's no other way of quenching the fire in her flabber chops.

Exit RAG

But my dear landlady, have a little patience.

LANDLADY   Patience! I scorn your words, Sir, is this a place to trust in? Tell me of patience, that used to have my money beforehand. Come, come, pay me quickly, or old Gregory Grime's house shall be too hot to hold you.

GAYMAN   Is't come to this, can I not be heard?

LANDLADY   No, Sir, you had good clothes when you came first, but they dwindled daily, till they dwindled to this old campaign, with tanned coloured lining, once red, but now all colours of the rainbow, a cloak to skulk in a-nights, and a pair of piss-burned shammy breeches. Nay, your very badge of manhood's gone too.

GAYMAN   How, landlady! Nay then i'faith no wonder if you rail so.

LANDLADY   Your silver sword I mean, transmogrified to this two-handed basket hilt, this old Sir Guy of Warwick, which will sell for nothing but old iron. In fine, I'll have my money, Sir, or i'faith Alsatia shall not shelter you.

Enter RAG

GAYMAN   Well, landlady, if we must part, let's drink at parting. Here, landlady, here's to the fool that shall love you better than I have done. (*Sighing, he drinks*)

LANDLADY   Rot your wine, d'ye think to pacify me with wine, Sir?

She refuses to drink. He holds open her jaws and RAG *throws a glass of wine into her mouth*

What, will you force me? No, give me another glass, I scorn to be so uncivil to be forced. My service to you, Sir. This shan't do, Sir.

She drinks. He, embracing her, sings

> Ah Cloris, 'tis in vain you scold.
> Whilst your eyes kindle such a fire,
> Your railing cannot make me cold,
> So fast as they a warmth inspire.

LANDLADY   Well Sir, you have no reason to complain of my eyes, nor my tongue neither, if rightly understood. (*Weeps*)

GAYMAN   I know you are the best of landladies, as such I drink your health. (*He drinks*) But to upbraid a man in tribulation. . . fie, 'tis not done like a woman of honour, a man that loves you too.

LANDLADY   I am a little hasty sometimes, but you know my good nature. (*She drinks*)

GAYMAN   I do, and therefore trust my little wants with you. I shall be rich again, and then my dearest landlady. . .

LANDLADY   Would this wine might ne'er go through me if I would not go, as they say, through fire and water, by night or by day for you. (*She drinks*)

GAYMAN   And as this is wine, I do believe thee. (*He drinks*)

LANDLADY   Well, you have no money in your pocket now, I'll warrant you; here, here's ten shillings for you old Gregory knows not of.

She opens a great greasy purse

GAYMAN   I cannot in conscience take it, good faith, I cannot. Besides, the next quarrel you'll hit me in the teeth with it.

LANDLADY   Nay, pray no more of that; forget it, forget it. I own I was to blame. Here Sir, you shall take it.

GAYMAN   Ay, but what should I do with money in these damned breeches! No, put it up, I can't appear thus. No, I'll stay at home, and lose my business.

LANDLADY   Why, is there no way to redeem one of your suits?

GAYMAN   None, none, I'll e'en lay me down and die.

LANDLADY   Die, marry, Heaven forbid, I would not for the world. Let me see, hum, what does it lie for?

GAYMAN   Alas dear landlady, a sum, a sum.

LANDLADY   Well, say no more, I'll lay about me.

GAYMAN   By this kiss but you shall not. . . (Assafetida, by this light.)

LANDLADY   Shall not? That's a good one, i'faith. Shall you rule, or I?

GAYMAN   But should your husband know it?

LANDLADY   Husband, marry come up, husbands know wives' secrets? No, sure, the world's not so bad yet. Where do your things lie? And for what?

GAYMAN   Five pounds equips me. Rag can conduct you, but I say you shall not go. I've sworn. . .

LANDLADY   Meddle with your matters; let me see, the caudle cup that Molly's grandmother left her will pawn for about that sum. I'll sneak it out. Well, Sir, you shall have your things presently, trouble not your head, but expect me.

Exeunt LANDLADY *and* RAG

GAYMAN   Was ever man put to such beastly shifts? S'death how she stank, my senses are most luxuriously regaled, there's my perpetual music too. . . (*Knocking of hammers on an anvil*) The ringing of bells is an ass to't.

Enter RAG

RAG   Sir, there's one in a coach below would speak to you.

GAYMAN   With me, and in a coach! Who can it be?

RAG   The Devil, I think, for he has a strange countenance.

GAYMAN   The Devil! Show yourself a rascal of parts, Sirrah, and wait on him up with ceremony.

RAG   Who, the Devil, Sir—?

GAYMAN   Ay, the Devil, Sir, if you mean to thrive.

Exit RAG

Who can this be? But see, he comes to inform me. Withdraw.

Enter BREDWELL *dressed like a devil*

BREDWELL   I come to bring you this. . . (*Gives him a letter*)

GAYMAN (*reads*)

'Receive what love and fortune present you with, be grateful and be silent, or 'twill vanish like a dream, and leave you more wretched than it found you.

Adieu'

Hah. . . (*Gives him a bag of money*)

BREDWELL   Nay view it, Sir, 'tis all substantial gold.

GAYMAN   (Now dare not I ask one civil question for fear it vanish all.) But I may ask, how 'tis I ought to pay for this great bounty.

BREDWELL   Sir, all the pay is secrecy.

GAYMAN   And is this all that is required, Sir?

BREDWELL   No, you're invited to the shades below.

GAYMAN   Hum, shades below! I am not prepared for such a journey, Sir.

BREDWELL   If you have courage, youth or love, you'll follow me: (*In feigned heroic tone*)

When night's black curtain's drawn around the world,

And mortal's eyes are safely locked in sleep,

And no bold spy dares view when Gods caress,

Then I'll conduct thee to the banks of bliss.

Durst thou not trust me?

GAYMAN   Yes, sure, on such substantial security. (*Hugs the bag*)

BREDWELL   Just when the day is vanished into night,

And only twinkling stars inform the world,

Near to the corner of the silent wall,

In fields of Lincoln's-Inn, thy spirit shall meet thee.

Farewell.

Exit BREDWELL

GAYMAN   Hum, I am awake, sure, and this is gold I grasp.

I could not see this devil's cloven foot;

Nor am I such a coxcomb to believe

But he was as substantial as his gold.

Spirits, ghosts, hobgoblins, furies, fiends and devils,

I've often heard old wives fright fools and children with,

Which, once arrived to common sense, they laugh at.

No, I am for things possible and natural:

Some female devil, old and damned to ugliness,

And past all hopes of courtship and address,

Full of another devil called desire,

Has seen this face, this shape, this youth,

And thinks it's worth her hire. It must be so.

I must moil on in the damned dirty road,

And sure, such pay will make the journey easy,
And for the price of the dull, drudging night,
All day I'll purchase new and fresh delight.

Exit GAYMAN

SCENE II

SIR FEEBLE'S HOUSE

Enter LETICIA, *pursued by* PHILLIS

PHILLIS   Why, Madam, do you leave the garden, for this retreat to
melancholy?
LETICIA   Because it suits my fortune and my humour; and even thy
presence would afflict me now.
PHILLIS   Madam, I was sent after you. My lady Fulbank has challenged
Sir Feeble at bowls, and stakes a ring of fifty pound against his new
chariot.
LETICIA   Tell him I wish him luck in everything but in his love to me.
Go tell him I am viewing of the garden.

Exit PHILLIS

Blessed be this kind retreat, this 'lone occasion
That lends a short cessation to my torments,
And gives me leave to vent my sighs and tears. (*Weeps*)

Enter BELLMOUR *at a distance behind her*

BELLMOUR   And doubly blessed be all the powers of love,
That gave me this dear opportunity.
LETICIA   Where were you, all ye pitying Gods of love,
That once seemed pleased at Bellmour's flame and mine,
And, smiling, joined our hearts, our sacred vows,
And spread your wings, and held your torches high?
BELLMOUR   Oh. . . (*She starts, and pauses*)
LETICIA   Where were you now, when this unequal marriage
Gave me from all my joys, gave me from Bellmour;
Your wings were flaged, your torches bent to earth,
And all your little bonnets veiled your eyes;
You saw not, or were deaf and pitiless.
BELLMOUR   Oh my Leticia!
LETICIA   Hah, 'tis there again; that very voice was Bellmour's.
Where art thou, oh thou lovely charming shade?
For sure, thou canst not take a shape to fright me.
What art thou?. . . speak!

Not looking behind her yet, for fear

BELLMOUR   Thy constant true adorer, who all this fatal day has
haunted thee to ease his tortured soul. (*Approaching her*)

LETICIA   (*speaking with signs of fear*)
My heart is well acquainted with that voice,
But, oh, my eyes dare not encounter thee.

BELLMOUR   Is it because thou'st broken all thy vows?
Take to thee courage, and behold thy slaughters.

LETICIA   Yes, though the sight would blast me, I would view it.
(*Turns*) 'Tis he, 'tis very Bellmour! or so like. . .
I cannot doubt but thou deserv'st this welcome. (*Embraces him*)

BELLMOUR   Oh my Leticia!

LETICIA   I'm sure I grasp not air; thou art no phantom.
My arms return not empty to my bosom,
But meet a solid treasure.

BELLMOUR   A treasure thou so easily threw'st away;
A riddle simple love ne'er understood.

LETICIA   Alas, I heard, my Bellmour, thou wert dead.

BELLMOUR   And was it thus you mourned my funeral?

LETICIA   I will not justify my hated crime.
But, oh, remember I was poor and helpless,
And much reduced, and much imposed upon. (BELLMOUR *weeps*)

BELLMOUR   And want compelled thee to this wretched marriage. . .
did it?

LETICIA   'Tis not a marriage, since my Bellmour lives;
The consummation were adultery.
I was thy wife before, would thou deny me?

BELLMOUR   No, by those powers that heard our mutual vows,
Those vows that tie us faster than dull priests.

LETICIA   But, oh my Bellmour, thy sad circumstances
Permit thee not to make a public claim.
Thou art proscribed, and diest if thou art seen.

BELLMOUR   Alas!

LETICIA   Yet I would wander with thee o'er the world,
And share thy humblest fortune with thy love.

BELLMOUR   Is't possible, Leticia, thou would'st fly
To foreign shores with me?

LETICIA   Can Bellmour doubt the soul he knows so well?

BELLMOUR   Perhaps in time the King may find my innocence, and
may extend his mercy. Meantime I'll make provision for our flight.

LETICIA   But how 'twixt this and that can I defend myself from the
loathèd arms of an impatient dotard, that I may come a spotless maid
to thee?

BELLMOUR   Thy native modesty and my industry
Shall well enough secure us.

Feign your nice virgin-cautions all the day;
Then trust at night to my conduct to preserve thee.
And wilt thou yet be mine? Oh, swear anew,
Give me again thy faith, thy vows, thy soul,
For mine's so sick with this day's fatal business,
It needs a cordial of that mighty strength;
Swear, swear, so as if thou break'st
Thou may'st be anything but damned, Leticia.

LETICIA   Thus then, and hear me, Heaven! (*Kneels*)
BELLMOUR   And thus, I'll listen to thee. (*Kneels*)

Enter SIR FEEBLE, LADY FULBANK *and* SIR CAUTIOUS

SIR FEEBLE   Lette, Lette, Lette, where are you, little rogue, Lette?
Hah, hum, what's here. . . ?

BELLMOUR *snatches her to his bosom, as if she fainted*

BELLMOUR   Oh Heavens, she's gone, she's gone!
SIR FEEBLE   Gone, whither is she gone? It seems she had the wit to
take good company with her.

The women go to her, and take her up

BELLMOUR   She's gone to Heaven, Sir, for ought I know.
SIR CAUTIOUS   She was resolved to go in a young fellow's arms, I see.
SIR FEEBLE   Go to, Francis, go to.
LADY FULBANK   Stand back, Sir, she recovers.
BELLMOUR   Alas, I found her dead upon the floor.
I should have left her so if I had known your mind.
SIR FEEBLE   Was it so, was it so? Got so, by no means, Francis?
LETICIA   Pardon him Sir, for surely I had died, but for his timely
coming.
SIR FEEBLE   Alas, poor pupsey, was it sick? Look here, here's a fine
thing to make it well again. Come buss, and it shall have it. Oh, how
I long for night. Ralph, are the fiddlers ready?
RALPH   They are tuning in the hall, Sir.
SIR FEEBLE   That's well, they know my mind. I hate that same twang,
twang, twang, fum, fum, tweedle, tweedle, tweedle, then screw go
the pins, till a man's teeth are on edge, then 'snap' says a small gut, and
there we are at a loss again. I long to be in bed with a hey tredodle,
tredodle, tredodle, with a hey tredool, tredodle, tredo. . . (*Dancing and
playing on his stick like a flute*)
SIR CAUTIOUS   A prudent man would reserve himself. Good-sacks, I
danced so on my wedding-day, that when I came to bed, to my shame
be it spoken, I fell fast asleep, and slept till morning.
LADY FULBANK   Where was your wisdom then, Sir Cautious? But I
know what a wise woman ought to have done.

SIR FEEBLE   Odsbobs, that's wormwood, that's wormwood. I shall have my young hussy set a-gog too. She'll hear there are better things in the world than she has at home, and then, odsbobs, and then they'll ha't, adod they will, Sir Cautious. Ever while you live, keep a wife ignorant, unless a man be as brisk as his neighbours.

SIR CAUTIOUS   A wise man will keep 'em from bawdy christ'nings then, and gossipings.

SIR FEEBLE   Christ'nings and gossipings! Why, they are the very schools that debauch our wives, as dancing-schools do our daughters.

SIR CAUTIOUS   Ay, when the overjoyed good man invites 'em all against that time twelve-month: 'Oh he's a dear man', cries one; 'I must marry', cries another; 'here's a man indeed, my husband, God help him'.

SIR FEEBLE   Then he falls to telling of her grievance, till (half maudlin) she weeps again. 'Just my condition,' cries a third. So the frolic goes round, and we poor cuckolds are anatomised, and turned the right side outwards; adsbobs, we are, Sir Cautious.

SIR CAUTIOUS   Ay, ay, this grievance ought to be redressed, Sir Feeble. The grave and sober part o'th' nation are hereby ridiculed. Ay, and cuckolded, too, for ought I know.

LADY FULBANK   Wise men knowing this, should not expose their infirmities, by marrying us young wenches, who, without instruction, find how we are imposed upon.

Enter fiddlers, playing, MR BEARJEST *and* DIANA *dancing,* BREDWELL *and* NOISEY, *etc.*

LADY FULBANK   So, Cousin, I see you have found the way to Mrs. Dy's heart.

BEARJEST   Who, I, my dear Lady Aunt? I never knew but one way to a woman's heart, and that road I have not yet travelled. For my uncle, who is a wise man, says matrimony is a sort of a. . . kind of a, as it were, d'ye see, of a voyage, which every man of fortune is bound to make one time or other, and Madam, I am, as it were, a bold adventurer.

DIANA   And are you sure, Sir, you will venture on me?

BEARJEST   Sure, I thank you for that, as if I could not believe my uncle, for in this case a young heir has no more to do, but to come and see, settle, marry, and use you scurvily.

DIANA   How, Sir, scurvily?

BEARJEST   Very scurvily, that is to say, be always fashionably drunk, despise the tyranny of your bed, and reign absolutely; keep a seraglio of women, and let my bastard issue inherit; be seen once a quarter, or so, with you in the park for countenance, where we loll two several ways in the gilt coach like Fanus, or a spread-eagle.

DIANA   And do you expect I should be honest the while?

BEARJEST   Heaven forbid, not I, I have not met with that wonder in all my travels.

LADY FULBANK   How, Sir, not an honest woman?

BEARJEST   Except my Lady Aunt. Nay, as I am a gentleman and the first of my family, you shall pardon me, here, cuff me soundly. (*Kneels to her*)

Enter GAYMAN, *richly dressed*

GAYMAN   This love's a damned bewitching thing. Now, though I should lose my assignation with my devil, I cannot hold from seeing Julia tonight. Hah! There! And with a fop at her feet. Oh vanity of woman! (*Softly pulls her*)

LADY FULBANK   Oh Sir, you're welcome from Northamptonshire.

GAYMAN   (Hum, surely she knows the cheat.)

LADY FULBANK   You are so gay, you save me, Sir, the labour of asking if your uncle be alive.

GAYMAN   (Pray heaven she have not found my circumstances! But if she have, confidence must assist me.)
And, Madam, you're too gay for me to inquire
Whether you are that Julia which I left you?

LADY FULBANK   Oh doubtless, Sir. . .

GAYMAN   But why the devil do I ask? Yes, you are still the same: one of those hoiting ladies, that love nothing like fool and fiddle, crowds of fops, had rather be publicly though dully flattered than privately adored. You love to pass for the wit of the company, by talking all and loud.

LADY FULBANK   Rail on, till you have made me think my virtue at so low ebb it should submit to you.

GAYMAN   What, I'm not discreet enough.
I'll babble all in my next high debauch;
Boast of your favours, and describe your charms
To every wishing fool.

LADY FULBANK   Or make most filthy verses of me
Under the name of Cloris, you Philander,
Who, in lewd rhymes, confess the dear appointment,
What hour, and where, how silent was the night,
How full of love your eyes, and wishing mine.
Faith, no. If you can afford me a lease of your love
Till the old gentleman my husband depart this wicked world,
I'm for the bargain.

SIR CAUTIOUS   Hum, what's here, a young spark at my wife? (*Goes about them*)

GAYMAN   Unreasonable Julia, is that all
My love, my sufferings, and my vows must hope?
Set me an age, say when you will be kind,

And I will languish out in starving wish;
But thus to gape for legacies of love,
Till youth be past enjoyment,
The devil I will as soon. Farewell. (*Offers to go*)

LADY FULBANK   Stay, I conjure you, stay.

GAYMAN   (And lose my assignation with my devil.)

SIR CAUTIOUS   'Tis so, ay, ay. 'Tis so, and wise men will perceive it. 'Tis here, here in my forehead. It more than buds, it sprouts, it flourishes.

SIR FEEBLE   So, that young gentleman has nettled him, stung him to the quick. I hope he'll chain her up, the gad-bee's in his conundrum. In charity I'll relieve him. Come my Lady Fulbank, the night grows old upon our hands; to dancing, to jiggiting, come. Shall I lead your Ladyship?

LADY FULBANK   No, Sir, you see I am better provided. . . (*Takes GAYMAN's hand*)

SIR CAUTIOUS   Ay, no doubt on't, a pox on him for a young handsome dog. (*They all dance*)

SIR FEEBLE   Very well, very well, now the posset, and then, ods bobs, and then. . .

DIANA   And then we'll have t'other dance.

SIR FEEBLE   Away girls, away, and steal the bride to bed; they have a deal to do upon their wedding nights, and what with the tedious ceremonies of dressing and undressing, the smutty lectures of the women by way of instruction, and the little stratagems of the young wenches, ods bobs, a man's cozen'd of half his night. Come gentlemen, one bottle, and then we'll toss the stocking.

Exeunt all but LADY FULBANK *and* BREDWELL, *who are talking, and* GAYMAN

LADY FULBANK   But dost thou think he'll come?

BREDWELL   I do believe so, Madam.

LADY FULBANK   Be sure you contrive so he may not know whither, or to whom he comes.

BREDWELL   I warrant you, Madam, for our parts.

Exit BREDWELL.   GAYMAN *attempts to sneak out*

LADY FULBANK   How now? What? Departing?

GAYMAN   You are going to the bride-chamber.

LADY FULBANK   No matter, you shall stay. . .

GAYMAN   I hate to have you in a crowd.

LADY FULBANK   Can you deny me? Will you not give me one lone hour i'th' garden?

GAYMAN   Where we shall only tantalise each other with dull kissing, and part with the same appetite we met? No, Madam. Besides I have business.

LADY FULBANK   Some assignation, is it so indeed?

GAYMAN   Away! You cannot think me such a traitor. 'Tis most important business.

LADY FULBANK   Oh, 'tis too late for business, let tomorrow serve.

GAYMAN   By no means; the gentleman is to go out of town.

LADY FULBANK   Rise the earlier then. . .

GAYMAN   But, Madam, the gentleman lies dangerously sick, and should he die. . .

LADY FULBANK   'Tis not a dying uncle, I hope, Sir?

GAYMAN   Hum.

LADY FULBANK   The gentleman a-dying, and to go out of town tomorrow?

GAYMAN   Ay, he goes in a litter. 'Tis his fancy, Madam. Change of air may recover him.

LADY FULBANK   So may your change of mistress do me, Sir, farewell

Exit LADY FULBANK

GAYMAN   Stay, Julia. Devil be damned, for you shall tempt no more. I'll love and be undone. But she is gone and if I stay the most that I shall gain is but a reconciling look, or kiss. . . No, my kind goblin, I'll keep my word with thee, as the least evil;
A tantalizing woman's worse than devil.

ACT III

SCENE I

SIR FEEBLE'S HOUSE

[*A song made by* MR CHEEK

No more, Lucinda, ah! expose no more
To the admiring world those conquering charms:
In vain all day unhappy men adore,
What the kind night gives to my longing arms.
Their vain attempts can ne'er successful prove,
Whilst I so well maintain the fort of love.

Yet to the world with so bewitching arts,
Your dazzling beauty you around display,
And triumph in the spoils of broken hearts
That sink beneath your feet, and crowd your way.
Ah! suffer now your cruelty to cease,
And to a fruitless war prefer a peace.]

Enter RALPH *with light,* SIR FEEBLE, *and* BELLMOUR, *sad*

SIR FEEBLE   So, so, they're gone. Come, Francis, you shall have the
honour of undressing me for the encounter; but 'twill be a sweet one,
Francis.

BELLMOUR   (Hell take him, how he teases me!) (*Undressing him all the
while*)

SIR FEEBLE   But is the young rogue laid, Francis, is she stolen to bed?
What tricks the young baggages have to whet a man's appetite!

BELLMOUR   Ay, Sir. (Pox on him, he will raise my anger up to
madness, and I shall kill him to prevent his going to bed to her.)

SIR FEEBLE   A piss of these bandstrings. The more haste, the less
speed.

BELLMOUR   (Be it so in all things, I beseech thee, Venus.)

SIR FEEBLE   Thy aid a little, Francis. (BELLMOUR *pinches him by
the throat*) Oh, oh thou chok'st me! 'Sbobs, what dost mean?

BELLMOUR   You had so hampered 'em, Sir. (The devil's very
mischievous in me.)

SIR FEEBLE   Come, come, quick, good Francis. Adod, I'm as yare as a
hawk at the young wanton. Nimbly, good Francis, untruss, untruss.

BELLMOUR   (Cramps seize ye. What shall I do? The near approach
distracts me.)

SIR FEEBLE   So, so, my breeches, good Francis. But well, Francis, how
dost think I got the young jade, my wife?

BELLMOUR   With five hundred pound a year jointure, Sir.

SIR FEEBLE   No, that would not do, the baggage was damnably in love
with a young fellow they call Bellmour, they say, that's truth on't;
and a pretty estate. But, happening to kill a man, he was forced to fly.

BELLMOUR   That was great pity, Sir.

SIR FEEBLE   Pity! Hang him, rogue, 'sbobs, and all the young fellows
in the town deserve it. We can never keep our wives and daughters
honest for rampant young dogs, and an old fellow cannot put in
amongst 'em , under being undone, with presenting, and the devil and
all. But what dost think I did? Being damnably in love, I feigned a
letter as from the Hague, wherein was a relation of this same Bellmour's
being hanged.

BELLMOUR   Is't possible, Sir, you could devise such news?

SIR FEEBLE   Possible, man! I did it, I did it! She swooned at the
news, shut herself up a whole month in her chamber, but I presented
high. She sighed and wept, and swore she'd never marry: still I
presented. She hated, loathed, spat upon me: still, adod, I presented.
Till I presented myself effectually in church to her, for she at last
wisely considered her vows were cancelled since Bellmour was hanged.

BELLMOUR   Sir, this was very cruel, to take away his fame, and then
his mistress.

SIR FEEBLE   Cruel! Thou'rt an ass! We are but even with the brisk
rogues, for they take away our fame, cuckold us, and take away our
wives. So, so, my cap, Francis.

BELLMOUR   And do you think this marriage lawful, Sir?

SIR FEEBLE   Lawful! It shall be when I've had livery and seisin of her
body, and that shall be presently, rogue, quick. Besides, this Bellmour
dares as well be hanged as come into England.

BELLMOUR   If he gets his pardon, Sir.

SIR FEEBLE   Pardon! No, no, I have took care for that, for I have,
you must know, got his pardon already.

BELLMOUR   How, Sir! Got his pardon. That's some amends for
robbing him of his wife.

SIR FEEBLE   Hold, honest Francis. What, dost think 'twas in
kindness to him? No, you fool, I got his pardon myself, that nobody
else should have it, so that if he gets anybody to speak to his Majesty
for it, his Majesty cries he has granted it. But for want of my
appearance he's defunct, trussed up, hanged, Francis.

BELLMOUR   This is the most excellent revenge I ever heard of.

SIR FEEBLE   Ay, I learnt it of a great politician of our times.

BELLMOUR   But have you got his pardon?

SIR FEEBLE   I've done't, I've done't. Pox on him, it cost me five
hundred pounds, though. Here 'tis. My solicitor brought it me this
evening. (*Gives it him*)

BELLMOUR   (This was a lucky hit, and if it 'scape me, let me be
hanged by a trick indeed.)

SIR FEEBLE   So, put it into my cabinet, safe, Francis, safe.

BELLMOUR   Safe, I'll warrant you, Sir.

SIR FEEBLE   My gown, quick, quick, t'other sleeve, man. So now my
night-cap. Well, I'll in, throw open my gown to fright away the
women, and jump into her arms.

Exit SIR FEEBLE

BELLMOUR   He's gone. Quickly, oh love, inspire me!

Enter a FOOTMAN

FOOTMAN   Sir, my master, Sir Cautious Fulbank, left his watch on
the little parlour table tonight, and bid me call for't.

BELLMOUR   Hah, the bridegroom has it, Sir, who is just gone to bed.
It shall be sent him in the morning.

FOOTMAN   'Tis very well, Sir, your servant.

Exit FOOTMAN

BELLMOUR   Let me see. Here is the watch, I took it up to keep for
him. But his sending has inspired me with a sudden stratagem that

will do better than force to secure the poor trembling Leticia, who,
I am sure, is dying with her fears.

Exit BELLMOUR

SCENE II

THE BEDCHAMBER

LETICIA *undressing by the women at the table. Enter* SIR FEEBLE
FAINWOOD

SIR FEEBLE   What's here? What's here? The prating women still. Ods
  bobs, what, not in bed yet, for shame of love, Leticia?
LETICIA   For shame of modesty, Sir. You would not have me go to
  bed before all this company.
SIR FEEBLE   What, the women! Why, they must see you laid.
  'Tis the fashion.
LETICIA   What, with a man? I would not for the world. (Oh Bellmour,
  where art thou with all thy promised aid?)
DIANA   Nay, Madam, we should see you laid indeed.
LETICIA   First in my grave, Diana.
SIR FEEBLE   Ods bobs, here's a compact amongst the women — high
  treason against the bridegroom — therefore ladies, withdraw, or adod
  I'll lock you all in. (*He throws open his gown; they run away, he locks
  the door*) So, so, now we're alone, Leticia. Off with this foolish
  modesty, and night-gown, and slide into my arms. (*She runs from
  him*) H'e' my little puskin. What, fly me, my coy Daphne? (*He
  pursues her. Knocking is heard*) Hah, who's that knocks, who's
  there?
BELLMOUR   'Tis I, Sir, 'tis I, open the door presently.
SIR FEEBLE   Why, what's the matter, is the house o-fire?
BELLMOUR   Worse Sir, worse.
LETICIA   ('Tis Bellmour's voice!)

  SIR FEEBLE *opens the door.* BELLMOUR *enters with the watch in
  his hand*

BELLMOUR   Oh Sir, do you know this watch?
SIR FEEBLE   This watch!
BELLMOUR   Ay Sir, this watch?
SIR FEEBLE   This watch! Why prithee, why dost tell me of a watch?
  'Tis Sir Cautious Fulbank's watch. What then, what a pox dost
  trouble me with watches? (SIR FEEBLE *attempts to eject*
  BELLMOUR, *who returns immediately*)

BELLMOUR   'Tis indeed his watch, Sir, and by this token he has sent
  for you to come immediately to his house, Sir.
SIR FEEBLE   What a devil. . . art mad, Francis? Or is His Worship mad,
  or does he think me mad? Go, prithee tell him I'll come tomorrow.
  (SIR FEEBLE *continues his attempt to put him out*)
BELLMOUR   Tomorrow, Sir! Why all our throats may be cut before
  we go to him tomorrow.
SIR FEEBLE   What say'st thou, throats cut?
BELLMOUR   Why, the City's up in arms, Sir, and all the aldermen
  are met at Guildhall; some damnable plot, Sir.
SIR FEEBLE   Hah, plot, the aldermen met at Guildhall! Hum! Why,
  let 'em meet, I'll not lose this night to save the nation.
LETICIA   Would you to bed, Sir, when the weighty affairs of state
  require your presence?
SIR FEEBLE   Hum, met at Guildhall. My clothes, my gown again,
  Francis, I'll out, out! What, upon my wedding night? No, I'll in.
  (SIR FEEBLE, *putting on his gown, pauses, pulls it off again*)
LETICIA   For shame, Sir, shall the reverend council of the city debate
  without you?
SIR FEEBLE   Ay, that's true, that's true. Come, truss again, Francis,
  truss again. Yet, now I think on't, Francis, prithee run thee to the
  hall, and tell 'em 'tis my wedding-night, d'ye see, Francis, and let
  somebody give my voice for. . .
BELLMOUR   What, Sir?
SIR FEEBLE   Adod, I cannot tell. Up in arms, say you! Why, let 'em
  fight. Dog fight bear, mun, I'll to bed. Go!
LETICIA   And shall his Majesty's service and safety lie unregarded for
  a slight woman, Sir?
SIR FEEBLE   Hum, his Majesty! Come, haste, Francis, I'll away. And
  call Ralph, and the footmen, and bid 'em arm; each man shoulder
  his musket and advance his pike, and bring my artillery impliments
  quick, and let's away. Pupsey, I'll bring it a fine thing yet before
  morning, it may be. Let's away: I shall grow fond and forget the
  business of the nation. Come, follow me, Francis.

Exit SIR FEEBLE. BELLMOUR *runs to* LETICIA

BELLMOUR   Now my Leticia, if thou e'er didst love,
  If ever thou design'st to make me blest
  Without delay fly this adulterous bed.
SIR FEEBLE   (*within*) Why, Francis, where are you, knave?
BELLMOUR   I must be gone lest he suspect us. I'll lose him and return
  to thee immediately. Get thyself ready.
LETICIA   I will not fail, my love.

Exit BELLMOUR

Old man, forgive me, thou the aggressor art,
Who rudely forced the hand without the heart.
She cannot from the paths of honour rove,
Whose guide's religion, and whose end is love.

Exit LETICIA

SCENE III

A WASH-HOUSE, OR OUT-HOUSE

Enter BREDWELL, *disguised like a devil, with a dark lantern, leading* GAYMAN

BREDWELL   Stay here till I give notice of your coming.

Exit BREDWELL, *leaving his dark lantern*

GAYMAN   Kind light, a little of your aid. Now must I be peeping, though my curiosity should lose me all. Hah, zouns, what's here, a hovel or a hog-sty? Hum, see the wickedness of man, that I should find no time to swear in, but just when I'm in the devil's clutches.

Enter PERT, *dressed as an old woman, with a staff*

PERT   Good even to you, fair Sir.
GAYMAN   Ha, defend me! If this be she, I must rival the Devil, that's certain.
PERT   Come, young gentleman, dare not you venture?
GAYMAN   (He must be as hot as Vesuvius that does. I shall never earn my morning's present.)
PERT   What, do you fear a longing woman, Sir?
GAYMAN   (The devil I do, this is a damned preparation to love.)
PERT   Why stand you gazing, Sir? A woman's passion is like the tide, it stays for no man when the hour is come.
GAYMAN   (I'm sorry I have took it at its turning; I'm sure mine's ebbing out as fast.)
PERT   Will you not speak, Sir? Will you not on?
GAYMAN   I would fain ask a civil question or two first.
PERT   You know too much curiosity lost paradise.
GAYMAN   Why, there's it now.
PERT   Fortune and love invite you, if you dare follow me.
GAYMAN   (This is the first thing in petticoats that ever dared me in vain. Were I but sure she were but human now, for sundry considerations she might down, but I will on.)

She goes, he follows

SCENE IV

A CHAMBER IN THE APARTMENT OF LADY FULBANK

Enter PERT, *followed by* GAYMAN *in the dark. Soft music plays.*
She leaves him

GAYMAN   Hah, Music, and excellent!

[SINGER

> *Oh! Love, that stronger art than wine,*
> *Pleasing delusion, witchery divine,*
> *Wont to be praised above all wealth,*
> *Disease that has more joys than health:*
> *Though we blaspheme thee in our pain,*
> *And of thy tyranny complain,*
> *We all are bettered by thy reign.*
>
> *What reason never can bestow,*
> *We to this useful passion owe.*
> *Love wakes the dull from sluggish ease,*
> *And learns a clown the art to please:*
> *Humbles the vain, kindles the cold,*
> *Makes misers free, and cowards bold.*
> *'Tis he reforms the sot from drink,*
> *And teaches airy fops to think.*
>
> *When full brute appetite is fed,*
> *And choked the glutton lies, and dead,*
> *Thou new spirits dost dispense,*
> *And find'st the gross delights of sense,*
> *Virtue's unconquerable aid,*
> *That against nature can persuade;*
> *And makes a roving mind retire*
> *Within the bounds of just desire.*
> *Cheerer of age, youth's kind unrest,*
> *And half the Heaven of the blest.*]

GAYMAN   Ah, Julia, Julia! If this soft preparation were but to bring
me to thy dear embraces, what different motions would surround my
soul from what perplex it now?

Enter nymphs and shepherds who dance. Then two dance alone. All
go out but PERT *and a* SHEPHERD

If these be devils they are obliging ones. I did not care if I ventured
on that last female fiend.

AT THE ROYAL COURT THIS SUMMER

AT THE ROYAL COURT

MINOR COMPLICATIONS
by Elisabeth Bond continues its successful run.

The cast includes Vincent Ebrahim, Souad Faress, Phyllis Logan,
Feroza Syal, Tony Wredden
Directed by Les Waters.

From August 2
ABEL'S SISTER
by Yolande Bourcier and Timberlake Wertenbaker

When Sandra, a young disabled woman, comes to the country to visit her
brother and his wife, she inevitably disturbs their comfortable, rational lives.
The appearance of Chris, a wounded American marine, complicates matters
further. As they all begin to contend with their own mutually exclusive
desires, no one is allowed to remain unscathed.
Directed by Les Waters
In conjunction with the Spastics Society.
With financial assistance from the Charities Aid Foundation.

IRISH FESTIVAL

An Irish Festival is scheduled for September/October comprising two new
plays about Ireland, (one in the Main House, the other in the Theatre
Upstairs), Irish music, poetry and a political debate.

MAIN STAGE   730 1745

From August 31
RAT IN THE SKULL
by Ron Hutchinson

Superintendent Harris would rather be at the bingo with the missus than in a
cell in Paddington Green trying to bottle up a case of police brutality. The
youthful and attractive P.C.Naylor, who may have witnessed the assault,
would rather be watching Spurs. And D.I.Nelson from the RUC would far
rather he'd stayed at home with his twenty-seven brothers all called Sam
than hit the suspect Michael Patrick de Valera Demon Bomber Roche in the
first place. Why did he disco on the Paddy's face? The Super thinks he
knows. The Constable knows he doesn't. Roche is saying nothing until he
finds all his teeth. Meanwhile, outside, the Paras prowl and the rubber bullets
hum . . .
Directed by Max Stafford-Clark

From September 5

The Theatre Upstairs presents Peter Cox's **Up to the Sun and Down to the
Centre** – the play which won him last year's George Devine Award. It is
based on a workshop held in Derry and concerns a mother's attempt to hold
her family, and herself together at an increasingly difficult time.
Directed by Danny Boyle

THE WOMENS PLAYHOUSE TRUST and
THE ROYAL COURT THEATRE
present

THE LUCKY CHANCE

by

Aphra Behn

in the first revival for more than 250 years

Cast:

Sir Cautious Fulbank	PAUL BACON
Lady Julia Fulbank	HARRIET WALTER
Gayman	ALAN RICKMAN
Sir Feeble Fainwould	JONATHAN ADAMS
Leticia Bredwell	KATHRYN POGSON
Bellmour	DENIS LAWSON
Bearjest	CHRISTOPHER FAIRBANK
Diana Fainwould	FRANCESCA BRILL
Bredwell	MARK TANDY
Fiddler/Gingle/Phillis/	PAM FERRIS
Ralph/Postman/Pert/	
Captain Noisey/Rag/	
Landlady/Dick/Parson	

The action of *The Lucky Chance* takes place over one
weekend in the summer of 1686.
There will be one interval of 15 minutes.

A Womens Playhouse Trust production with
the Royal Court Theatre
First performance at the Royal Court Theatre on 4th July 1984

Directed by	Jules Wright
Designed by	Jenny Tiramani
Music by	Ilona Sekacz
Lighting by	Geoffrey Joyce
Choreography by	Jacky Lansley
Fights arranged by	Malcolm Ranson
Assistant Director	Kate Harwood
Stage Manager	Jane Salberg
Deputy Stage Manager	Judi Wheway
Assistant Stage Manager	Rosie Cullen
Poster Design	Jane Gifford

For the Royal Court Theatre:

Front of House Manager	Richard Masterman
Casting Assistance	Simon Curtis
Publicity Manager	Sheila Fox (730 5174)
Publicity Assistant	Natasha Harvey

For the Womens Playhouse Trust:

Associate Director	Sue Parrish
General Manager	Rosemary Squire
Production Accountant	Candace Imison
Press	Joy Sapieka & Toni Racklin (741 9174)
Marketing	Celia Goulden & Flicky Ridel (359 8514)

The Womens Playhouse Trust wishes to thank Fidelis Morgan for the use of her edition of the text of *The Lucky Chance*, published by Virago Press Ltd, (1981), in the collection *The Female Wits: Women Playwrights of the Restoration*.

SUBSIDISED BY THE
Arts Council
OF GREAT BRITAIN

GLC
funded

THE WOMENS PLAYHOUSE TRUST

The Womens Playhouse Trust held its inaugural meeting at the House of Commons on 17 November 1981, and received charitable status in January 1983. The Trust was formed by a group of prominent people in the arts and public life to improve the opportunities in the theatre for women directors, designers, writers, actresses and technicians. It aims for the highest artistic standards and has impressive backing from the establishment and working actresses, because it is 'pragmatic, broad-based and visionary'.

'It is said that there is nothing so powerful as an idea whose time has come; and I have a hunch that the Trust is striking at the right moment'
Michael Billington, The Guardian, 2nd December 1983

President: Dame Peggy Ashcroft, DBE
Directors: Sue Parrish, Nicole Penn-Symons, Rosemary Squire, Jules Wright
Steering Group: Sheila Allen, Connie Borkenhagen, Sandra Brown, Pam Gems, Susi Hush, Glenda Jackson, Lady Jenkins, Miriam Karlin, Phil Kelvin, Manuela Kleeman, Jane Lapotaire, Lady Melchett, Diana Quick, Hilary Salmon, Pamela Stephenson, Elizabeth Thomas, Babs Todd
European Consultant: Renee Goddard

The Sarah Siddons Development Committee, chaired by Lady Harlech, was established to secure a permanent home for the WPT, to be named the Sarah Siddons Theatre.

Chairwoman: The Lady Harlech
Vice Presidents: The Countess of Airlie, The Rt. Hon. the Lord Harlech, The Marchioness of Lothian, The Princess Helena Moutafian, MBE, The Hon. Robert Rayne
Committee: Miss Maria Aitken, Mrs Susan Bernerd, Miss Anouska Hempel, Mrs Robert Rayne

The Lucky Chance is very generously funded by the GLC.

The WPT is indebted to the generosity of Blakes for sponsoring this production.

Thanks to the Royal Victoria Hall Foundation which has financially supported this production.

Special thanks to: Nicholas Baatz, R.J.Beecham, Susan Bernerd, Alan Brodie, Faith Brook, Stuart Burge, Anthony C. Burton, Peter Cadbury, Bernard Carnell & Liz Badger, City Women's Network, Sarah Cockburn, Mr & Mrs Andrew Cruickshank, Harriet Cruickshank, Jennifer d'Abo, Tessa Dahl, Eleanor and Martin Day, Gerald Divall, Jeremy Friend, Simon Frisby, Pam Gems, Lady Harlech, Angela Higgins, Michael Imison and staff, Tamsyn Imison, Miriam Karlin, Phil Kelvin, David & Manuela Kleeman, Peter Kleeman, Jane Lapotaire, Limehouse Pictures, Maureen Michaelson, Methuen London, Derek Morris, Patricia Negus Fancey, The Hon. & Mrs Robert Rayne, Angharad Rees, Martha Richards, D. Royce, Bernard Simons, Andrew Smith, Christina Smith, Mary & Donald Squire, Louise Stein, Sue Storr, John Tackaberry, Mr and Mrs Mark Weinberg, Nigel Wray, Geoffrey Wren, Josh Wright, Susannah York

The WPT gratefully acknowledges the support of Sheila Needham and Needham Printers Ltd for subsidising the printing of leaflets and posters for The Lucky Chance.

SHEPHERD

> *Cease your wonder, cease your guess,*
> *Whence arrives your happiness.*
> *Cease your wonder, cease your pain,*
> *Human fancy is in vain.*

CHORUS

> *'Tis enough, you once shall find,*
> *Fortune may to worth be kind;*
> *And love can leave off being blind.*

They give him gold

PERT

> *You, before you enter here*
> *On this sacred ring must swear,*

PERT *puts the ring on* GAYMAN's *finger, holds his hand*

> *By the figure which is round,*
> *Your passion constant and profound;*
> *By the Adamantine Stone,*
> *To be fixed to one alone:*
> *By the lustre, which is true,*
> *Ne'er to break your sacred vow.*
> *Lastly, by the gold that's tried,*
> *For love all dangers to abide.*

They all dance about him, while PERT *and* SHEPHERD *sing*

SHEPHERD

> *Once about him let us move,*
> *To confirm him true to love.*

PERT

> *Twice with mystic turning feet,*
> *Make him silent and discreet.*

SHEPHERD

> *Thrice about him let us tread,*
> *To keep him ever young in bed.*

SHEPHERD

> *Forget Aminta's proud disdain;*
> *Haste here, and sigh no more in vain,*
> *The joy of love without the pain.*

PERT

> *That God repents his former slights,*
> *And fortune thus your faith requites.*

BOTH

> Forget Aminta's proud disdain;
> Then taste, and sigh no more in vain,
> The joy of love without the pain,
> The joy of love without the pain.

Exeunt all dancers. GAYMAN *looks on himself, and feels about him*

GAYMAN   What the Devil can all this mean? If there be a woman in the case, sure I have not lived so bad a life to gain the dull reputation of so modest a coxcomb, but that a female might down with me without all this ceremony? Is it care of her honour? That cannot be; this age affords none so nice. Nor fiend nor goddess can she be, for these I saw were mortal. No, 'tis a woman, I am positive. Not young nor handsome, for then vanity had made her glory to have been seen. No, since 'tis resolved a woman, she must be old and ugly, and will not baulk my fancy with her sight, but baits me more with this essential beauty.
Well, be she young or old, woman or devil,
She pays, and I'll endeavour to be civil.

SCENE V

IN THE SAME HOUSE

After a knocking, enter BREDWELL *in his masking habit, with his vizard in the one hand, and a light in the other, in haste*

BREDWELL   Hah, knocking so late at our gate.

He opens the door. Enter SIR FEEBLE, *dressed, and armed from head to toe, with a broad waist-belt stuck round with pistols, a helmet, scarf, buff-coat and half-pike*

SIR FEEBLE   How now, how now, what's the matter here?
BREDWELL   Matter? (What, is my lady's innocent intrigue found out?) Heavens, Sir, what makes you here in this warlike equipage?
SIR FEEBLE   What makes you in this showing equipage, Sir?
BREDWELL   I have been dancing among some of my friends.
SIR FEEBLE   And I thought to have been fighting with some of my friends. Where's Sir Cautious? Where's Sir Cautious?
BREDWELL   Sir Cautious, Sir? In bed.
SIR FEEBLE   Call him, call him quickly, good Edward.
BREDWELL   (Sure, my lady's frolic is betrayed and he comes to make mischief. However, I'll go and secure Mr Gayman.)

Exit BREDWELL

Enter SIR CAUTIOUS *and* DICK *with light*

DICK   Pray, Sir, go to bed. Here's no thieves. All's still and well.

SIR CAUTIOUS   This last night's misfortune of mine, Dick, has kept me waking, and methought all night I heard a kind of a silent noise. I am still afraid of thieves. Mercy upon me to lose five hundred guineas at one clap, Dick. Hah, bless me! what's yonder? Blow the great horn, Dick! Thieves! Murder, murder!

SIR FEEBLE   Why, what a pox, are you mad? 'Tis I, 'tis I, man.

SIR CAUTIOUS   I, who am 'I'? Speak — declare — pronounce.

SIR FEEBLE   Your friend, old Feeble Fainwood.

SIR CAUTIOUS   How, Sir Feeble! (At this late hour, and on his wedding night.) Why, what's the matter Sir, is it peace or war with you?

SIR FEEBLE   A mistake, a mistake. Proceed to the business, good brother, for time is precious.

SIR CAUTIOUS   (Some strange catastrophe has happened between him and his wife tonight, and makes him disturb me thus.) Come, sit, good brother, and to the business, as you say.

They sit, one at one end of the table, the other at the other. DICK *sets down the light and goes out. Both sit gaping and staring and expecting when either should speak*

SIR FEEBLE   As soon as you please, Sir. (Lord, how wildly he stares! He's much disturbed in's mind.) Well Sir, let us be brief.

SIR CAUTIOUS   As brief as you please, Sir. Well, brother?

Pausing still

SIR FEEBLE   So, Sir.

SIR CAUTIOUS   (How strangely he stares and gapes — some deep concern.)

SIR FEEBLE   Hum. . . hum.

SIR CAUTIOUS   I listen to you, advance.

SIR FEEBLE   Sir?

SIR CAUTIOUS   (A very distracted countenance. Pray Heaven he be not mad, and a young wife is able to make an old fellow mad, that's the truth on't.)

SIR FEEBLE   (Sure, 'tis something of his lady, he's so loth to bring it out.) I am sorry you are thus disturbed, Sir.

SIR CAUTIOUS   No disturbance to serve a friend.

SIR FEEBLE   I think I am your friend indeed, Sir Cautious, or I would not have been here upon my wedding night.

SIR CAUTIOUS   (His wedding night, there lies his grief, poor heart! Perhaps she has cuckolded him already.) Well, come, brother, say such things are done.

SIR FEEBLE   Done, hum, come, out with it. Brother, what troubles you tonight?

SIR CAUTIOUS   (Troubles me? Why, knows he I am robbed?)

SIR FEEBLE   I may perhaps restore you to the rest you've lost.

SIR CAUTIOUS   The rest, why, have I lost more since? Why, know you then who did it? Oh, how I'd be revenged upon the rascal!

SIR FEEBLE   ('Tis jealousy, the old worm that bites.) Who is it you suspect?

SIR CAUTIOUS   Alas, I know not whom to suspect, I would I did; but if you could discover him I would so swinge him.

SIR FEEBLE   I know him. What, do you take me for a pimp, Sir? I know him — there's your watch again, Sir. I'm your friend, but no pimp, Sir. (SIR FEEBLE *rises in rage*)

SIR CAUTIOUS   My watch, I thank you, Sir, but why pimp, Sir?

SIR FEEBLE   Oh, a very thriving calling, Sir, and I have a young wife to practise with. I know your rogues.

SIR CAUTIOUS   A young wife! ('Tis so, his gentlewoman has been at hot cockles without her husband, and he's horn-mad upon it. I suspected her be so close in with his nephew, in a fit with a pox.) Come, come, Sir Feeble, 'tis many an honest man's fortune.

SIR FEEBLE   I grant it, Sir, but to the business, Sir, I came for.

SIR CAUTIOUS   With all my soul.

They sit gaping and expecting when either should speak. Enter BREDWELL and GAYMAN at the door. BREDWELL sees them and puts GAYMAN back again

BREDWELL   Hah, Sir Feeble and Sir Cautious there! What shall I do? For this way we must pass, and to carry him back would discover my lady to him, betray all, and spoil the jest. Retire, Sir, your life depends upon your being unseen.

They go out

SIR FEEBLE   Well, Sir, do you not know that I am married, Sir? And this my wedding night?

SIR CAUTIOUS   Very good, Sir.

SIR FEEBLE   And that I long to be in bed?

SIR CAUTIOUS   Very well, Sir.

SIR FEEBLE   Very good, Sir, and very well, Sir. Why then, what the Devil do I make here, Sir? (SIR FEEBLE *again rises in a rage*)

SIR CAUTIOUS   Patience, brother — and forward.

SIR FEEBLE   Forward! Lend me your hand, good brother, let's feel your pulse. How has this night gone with you?

SIR CAUTIOUS   Ha, ha, ha, this is the oddest conundrum. (Sure, he's mad, and yet, now I think on't, I have not slept tonight, nor shall I ever sleep again till I have found the villain that robbed me.)

(SIR CAUTIOUS *weeps*)

SIR FEEBLE   (So, now he weeps — far gone — this laughing and weeping is a very bad sign!) Come, let me lead you to your bed.

SIR CAUTIOUS   (Mad, stark mad.) No, now I'm up 'tis no matter, pray ease your troubled mind. I am your friend — out with it — what, was it acted, or but designed?

SIR FEEBLE   How, Sir?

SIR CAUTIOUS   Be not ashamed, I'm under the same predicament I doubt, little better than a. . . but let that pass.

SIR FEEBLE   Have you any proof?

SIR CAUTIOUS   Proof of what, good Sir?

SIR FEEBLE   Of what? Why, that you're a cuckold, Sir, a cuckold if you'll have it.

SIR CAUTIOUS   Cuckold! Sir, do ye know what ye say?

SIR FEEBLE   What I say?

SIR CAUTIOUS   Ay, what you say! Can you make this out?

SIR FEEBLE   I make it out!

SIR CAUTIOUS   Ay, Sir — if you say it, and cannot make it out, you're a. . .

SIR FEEBLE   What am I, Sir? What am I?

SIR CAUTIOUS   A cuckold as well as myself, Sir. And I'll sue you for Scandalum Magnatum. I shall recover swingeing damages with a City jury.

SIR FEEBLE   I know of no such thing, Sir.

SIR CAUTIOUS   No, Sir?

SIR FEEBLE   No, Sir.

SIR CAUTIOUS   Then what would you be at, Sir?

SIR FEEBLE   I be at, Sir! What would you be at, Sir?

SIR CAUTIOUS   Ha, ha, ha! Why, this is the strangest thing, to see an old fellow, a magistrate of the City, the first night he's married forsake his bride and bed and come armed, cap-à-pied, like Gargantua, to disturb another old fellow, and banter him with a tale of a tub, and all to be-cuckold him here! In plain English, what's your business?

SIR FEEBLE   Why, what the Devil's your business, and you go to that?

SIR CAUTIOUS   My business, with whom?

SIR FEEBLE   With me, Sir, with me. What a pox do you think I do here?

SIR CAUTIOUS   'Tis that I would be glad to know, Sir.

Enter DICK

SIR FEEBLE   Here, Dick, remember I've brought back your master's watch. Next time he sends for me o'er night, I'll come to him in the morning.

SIR CAUTIOUS   Ha, ha, ha, I send for you? Go home and sleep,

Sir, and ye keep your wife waking to so little purpose, you'll go near to be haunted with a vision of horn.

SIR FEEBLE   Roguery, knavery, to keep me from my wife — look ye, this was the message I received.

He goes to tell him. Enter BREDWELL *in a white sheet like a ghost, speaking to* GAYMAN *who stands within*

BREDWELL   Now, Sir, we are two to two, for this way you must pass to be taken in the lady's lodgings. I'll first adventure out to make you pass the safer (and that he may not, if possible, see Sir Cautious, whom I shall fright into a trance, I am sure. And Sir Feeble, the Devil's in it, if he know him).

GAYMAN   A brave kind fellow this.

BREDWELL, *stalking on as a ghost past the two old men*

SIR CAUTIOUS   Oh, undone, undone. Help, help! I'm dead, I'm dead!

SIR CAUTIOUS *falls down on his face.* SIR FEEBLE *stares and stands still*

BREDWELL   (As I could wish. Come on, thou ghastly thing, and follow me.)

Enter GAYMAN, *like a ghost, with a torch*

SIR CAUTIOUS   Oh, Lord! Oh, Lord!

GAYMAN   Hah! Old Sir Feeble Fainwood! Why, where the Devil am I? 'Tis he, and be it where it will I'll fright the old dotard for cozening my friend of his mistress. (GAYMAN *stalks on*)

SIR FEEBLE (*trembling*)   Oh guard me, guard me, all ye powers!

GAYMAN   Thou call'st in vain, fond wretch, for I am Bellmour,
Whom first thou robbed of fame and life,
And then what dearer was, his wife.

GAYMAN *goes out, shaking his torch at him*

SIR CAUTIOUS   Oh, Lord, Oh, Lord!

Enter LADY FULBANK *in an undress, and* PERT *undressed*

LADY FULBANK   Heavens, what noise is this? So he's got safe out, I see. (*Sees* SIR FEEBLE *armed*) Hah, what thing art thou?

SIR FEEBLE   Stay, Madam, stay — 'tis I, a poor trembling mortal.

LADY FULBANK   Sir Feeble Fainwood! Rise, are you both mad?

SIR CAUTIOUS   No, no, Madam, we have seen the Devil.

SIR FEEBLE   Ay, and he was as tall as the Monument!

SIR CAUTIOUS   With eyes like a beacon, and a mouth, Heaven bless us, like London Bridge at full tide.

SIR FEEBLE   Ay, and roared as loud.

LADY FULBANK   Idle fancies! What makes you from your bed, and you, Sir, from your bride?

SIR FEEBLE   Oh, that's the business of another day, a mistake only, Madam.

LADY FULBANK   Away, I'm ashamed to see wise men so weak — the phantoms of the night, or your own shadows, the whimsies of the brain for want of rest, or perhaps Bredwell, your Man, who, being wiser than his master, played you this trick to fright you both to bed.

SIR FEEBLE   Hum, adod, and that may be, for the young knave when he let me in tonight was dressed up for some waggery.

SIR CAUTIOUS   Ha, ha, ha, 'twas even so, sure enough, brother.

SIR FEEBLE   Ods bobs, but they frighted me at first basely. . . But I'll home to Pupsey. There may be roguery as well as here. Madam, I ask your pardon, I see we're all mistaken.

LADY FULBANK   Ay, Sir Feeble, go home to your wife.

SCENE VI

DARKNESS. THE STREET

Enter BELLMOUR. *He knocks at the door,* PHILLIS *opens it*

PHILLIS   Oh, are you come, Sir? I'll call my lady down.

BELLMOUR   Oh, haste, the minutes fly — leave all behind, and bring Leticia only to my arms.

A noise of people

Hah, what noise is that? 'Tis coming this way. I tremble with my fears, hah, death and the Devil, 'tis he.

Enter SIR FEEBLE *and his men, armed. He too goes to the door, and knocks*

Ay, 'tis he, and I'm undone — what shall I do to kill him now? Besides, the sin would put me past all hopes of pardoning.

SIR FEEBLE   A damned rogue to deceive me thus.

BELLMOUR   Hah — see, by Heaven, Leticia. Oh, we are ruined!

SIR FEEBLE   Hum, what's here, two women?

SIR FEEBLE *stands a little off. Enter* LETICIA *and* PHILLIS *softly, undressed, with a box*

LETICIA   Where are you, my best wishes? Lord of my vows, and charmer of my soul? Where are you?

BELLMOUR   Oh, Heavens! (*He draws his sword half-way*)

SIR FEEBLE   (Hum, who's here? My gentlewoman — she's monstrous kind of the sudden. But whom is't meant to?)

LETICIA   Give me your hand, my love, my life, my all. Alas! Where are you?

SIR FEEBLE   (Hum, no, no, this is not to me. I am jilted, cozened, cuckolded, and so forth.)

Groping, she takes hold of SIR FEEBLE

LETICIA   Oh, are you here? Indeed you frighted me with your silence — here, take these jewels and let us haste away.

SIR FEEBLE   (Hum, are you thereabouts, mistress? Was I sent away with a sham plot for this? She cannot mean it to me.)

LETICIA   Will you not speak? Will you not answer me? Do you repent already? Before enjoyment are you cold and false?

SIR FEEBLE   (Hum, before enjoyment, that must be me. Before enjoyment.) Ay, ay, 'tis I. (*Merrily*) (I see a little prolonging a woman's joy sets an edge upon her appetite.)

LETICIA   What means my dear? Shall we not haste away?

SIR FEEBLE   (Haste away! There 'tis again. No, 'tis not me she means) What, at your tricks and intrigues already? Yes, yes, I am destined a cuckold!

LETICIA   Say, am I not your wife? Can you deny me?

SIR FEEBLE (*merrily*)   Wife! adod 'tis I she means, 'tis I she means.

LETICIA   Oh, Bellmour, Bellmour!

SIR FEEBLE *starts back from her hands*

SIR FEEBLE   Hum, what's that, Bellmour?

LETICIA   Hah! Sir Feeble! He would not, Sir, have used me thus unkindly.

SIR FEEBLE   Oh, I'm glad 'tis no worse. (Bellmour quoth 'a! I thought the ghost was come again.)

PHILLIS   Why did you not speak, Sir, all this while? My lady weeps with your unkindness.

SIR FEEBLE   I did but hold my peace to hear how prettily she prattled love. But fags, you are naught to think of a young fellow, ads bobs, you are now.

LETICIA   I only say he would not have been so unkind to me.

SIR FEEBLE   But what makes ye out at this hour, and with these jewels?

PHILLIS   Alas, Sir, we thought the City was in arms, and packed up our things to secure 'em, if there had been a necessity for flight. For had they come to plundering once, they would have begun with the rich Aldermen's wives, you know, Sir.

SIR FEEBLE   Ads bobs, and so they would. But there was no arms, nor mutiny. Where's Francis?

BELLMOUR   Here, Sir.

SIR FEEBLE   Here, Sir! Why, what a story you made of a meeting in the hall, and arms, and — a — the Devil of anything was stirring, but a couple of old fools that sat gaping and waiting for one another's business.

BELLMOUR   Such a message was brought me, Sir.

SIR FEEBLE   Brought! Thou'rt an ass, Francis, but no more — come, come, let's to bed.

LETICIA   To bed, Sir! What, by daylight? For that's hasting on. I would not for the world — the night would hide my blushes, but the day. . . would let me see myself in your embraces.

SIR FEEBLE   Embraces, in a fiddlestick. Why, are we not married?

LETICIA   'Tis true, Sir, and time will make me more familiar with you, but yet my virgin modesty forbids it. I'll to Diana's chamber. The night will come again.

SIR FEEBLE   For once you shall prevail, and this damned jaunt has pretty well mortified me. A pox of your mutiny, Francis. Come, I'll conduct thee to Diana and lock thee in, that I may have thee safe, rogue. We'll give young wenches leave to whine and blush, And fly those blessings which, ads bobs, they wish.

ACT IV

SCENE I

SIR FEEBLE'S HOUSE

Enter LADY FULBANK, GAYMAN, *sighing and gently pulling her back by the hand.* RALPH *meets them*

LADY FULBANK   How now, Ralph, let your lady know I am come to wait on her.

Exit RALPH

GAYMAN   Oh, why this needless visit? Your husband's safe, at least till evening, safe. Why will you not go back and give me one soft hour, though to torment me?

LADY FULBANK   You are at leisure now, I thank you, Sir. Last night when I, with all love's rhetoric pleaded, and Heaven knows what last night might have produced, you were engaged! False man, I do believe it, and I am satisfied you love me not.

She walks away in scorn

GAYMAN   Not love you!
   Why do I waste my youth in vain pursuit,
   Neglecting interest, and despising power?
   Unheeding and despising other beauties.
   Why at your feet are all my fortunes laid,
   And why does all my fate depend on you?
LADY FULBANK   I'll not consider why you play the fool,
   Present me rings and bracelets, why pursue me,
   Why watch whole nights before my senseless door,
   And take such pains to show yourself a coxcomb.
GAYMAN   Oh! Why all this?
   By all the powers above, by this dear hand,
   And by this ring, which on this hand I place,
   On which I've sworn fidelity to love,
   I never had a wish or soft desire
   To any other woman
   Since Julia swayed the empire of my soul.
LADY FULBANK   (Hah, my own ring I gave him last night.)
   Your jewel, Sir, is rich.
   Why do you part with things of so much value
   So easily, and so frequently?
GAYMAN   To strengthen the weak arguments of love.
LADY FULBANK   And leave yourself undone?
GAYMAN   Impossible, if I am blessed with Julia.
LADY FULBANK   Love's a thin diet, nor will keep out cold.
   You cannot satisfy your dunning tailor
   To cry — I am in love! Though possibly you
   May your seamstress.
GAYMAN   Does ought about me speak such poverty?
LADY FULBANK   I am sorry that it does not, since to maintain this
   gallantry 'tis said you use base means, below a gentleman.
GAYMAN   Who dares but to imagine it is a rascal, a slave, below a
   beating. What means my Julia?
LADY FULBANK   No more dissembling, I know your land is gone.
   I know each circumstance of all your wants. Therefore, as e'er you
   hope that I should love you ever, tell me where 'twas you got this
   jewel, Sir.
GAYMAN   (Hah — I hope 'tis not stolen goods.) Why, on the sudden,
   all this nice examining?
LADY FULBANK   You trifle with me and I'll plead no more.
GAYMAN   Stay — why — I bought it, Madam —
LADY FULBANK   Where had you money, Sir? You see, I am no
   stranger to your poverty.
GAYMAN   This is strange, perhaps it is a secret.
LADY FULBANK   So is my love, which shall be kept from you.

She attempts to go

GAYMAN (*sighing*)   Stay, Julia — your will shall be obeyed.
　　Though I had rather die than be obedient,
　　Because I know you'll hate me when 'tis told.
LADY FULBANK   By all my vows, let it be what it will,
　　It ne'er shall alter me from loving you.
GAYMAN   I have, of late, been tempted, with presents, jewels, and
　　large sums of gold.
LADY FULBANK   Tempted? By whom?
GAYMAN   The Devil, for ought I know.
LADY FULBANK   Defend me, Heaven! the Devil? I hope you have
　　not made a contract with him.
GAYMAN   No, though in the shape of a woman it appeared.
LADY FULBANK   Where met you with it?
GAYMAN   By magic art I was conducted — I know not how,
　　To an enchanted palace in the clouds, where I was so attended —
　　Young dancing, singing fiends innumerable.
LADY FULBANK   Imagination, all!
GAYMAN   But for the amorous Devil, the old Proserpine —
LADY FULBANK   Ay, she, what said she?
GAYMAN   Not a word. Heaven be praised, she was a silent Devil, but
　　she was laid in a pavilion all formed of gilded clouds which hung by
　　geometry, whither I was conveyed after much ceremony, and laid in
　　a bed with her, where, with much ado and trembling with my fears,
　　I forced my arms about her.
LADY FULBANK   (And sure that undeceived him.)
GAYMAN   But such a carcass 'twas, deliver me, so shrivelled, lean
　　and rough, a canvas bag of wooden ladles were a better bedfellow.
LADY FULBANK   (Now, though I know that nothing is more distant
　　than I from such a monster, yet this angers me.) Death! could you
　　love me and submit to this?
GAYMAN   'Twas that first drew me in. The tempting hope of means
　　to conquer you, would put me upon any dangerous enterprise. Were
　　I the Lord of all the universe, I am so lost in love, for one dear night
　　to clasp you in my arms I'd lavish all that world, then die with joy.
LADY FULBANK   ('Slife, after all to seem deformed, old, ugly.)

She walks in a fret

GAYMAN   I knew you would be angry when you heard it.

He pursues her in a submissive posture. Enter SIR CAUTIOUS,
BEARJEST, NOISEY *and* BREDWELL

SIR CAUTIOUS   How, what's here? My lady with the spark that
　　courted her last night? Hum, with her again so soon? Well, this

impudence and importunity undoes more City wives than all their
unmerciful finery.

GAYMAN   But Madam —

LADY FULBANK   Oh, here's my husband, you'd best tell him your
story. (*Angrily*) What makes him here so soon?

SIR CAUTIOUS   (Me his story! I hope he will not tell me he's a mind
to cuckold me.)

GAYMAN   (A Devil on him, what shall I say to him?)

LADY FULBANK   (What, so excellent at intrigues, and so dull at an
excuse?)

GAYMAN   Yes, Madam, I shall tell him —

Enter BELLMOUR

LADY FULBANK   Is my lady at leisure for a visit, Sir?

BELLMOUR   Always, to receive your ladyship.

She goes out

SIR CAUTIOUS   With me, Sir, would you speak?

GAYMAN   With you, Sir, if your name be Fulbank.

SIR CAUTIOUS   Plain Fulbank! Methinks you might have had a
Sir-reverence under your girdle, Sir. I am honoured with another
title, Sir —

SIR CAUTIOUS *goes talking to the rest*

GAYMAN   With many, Sir, that very well becomes you —

GAYMAN *pulls* SIR CAUTIOUS *a little aside*

I've something to deliver to your ear.

SIR CAUTIOUS   (So, I'll be hanged if he do not tell me I'm a cuckold
now. I see it in his eyes.) My ear, Sir! I'd have you to know I scorn
any man's secrets, Sir, for aught I know you may whisper treason
to me, Sir. (Pox on him, how handsome he is, I hate the sight of the
young stallion.)

GAYMAN   I would not be so uncivil, Sir, before all this company.

SIR CAUTIOUS   Uncivil! (Ay, ay, 'tis so, he cannot be content to
cuckold, but he must tell me so, too.)

GAYMAN   But since you will have it, Sir, you are a rascal, a most
notorious villain, Sir, d'ye hear?

SIR CAUTIOUS (*laughing*)   Yes, yes, I do hear — and am glad 'tis no
worse.

GAYMAN   Griping as Hell, and as insatiable, worse than a brokering
Jew, not all the Twelve Tribes harbour such a damned extortioner.

SIR CAUTIOUS   Pray under favour, Sir, who are you?

GAYMAN (*pulling off his hat*)   One whom thou hast undone.

SIR CAUTIOUS (*smiling*)   (Hum — I'm glad of that, however.)

GAYMAN   Racking me up to starving want and misery, then took advantage to ruin me.

SIR CAUTIOUS (*smiling*)   (So, and he'd revenge it on my wife.)

GAYMAN   Do you not know one Wasteall, Sir?

Enter RALPH *with wine, sets it on a table*

SIR CAUTIOUS   Wasteall — ha, ha, ha — if you are any friend to that poor fellow you may return and tell him, Sir, d'ye hear, that the mortgage of two hundred pound a year is this day out, and I'll not bait him an hour, Sir — ha, ha, ha — what, do you think to hector civil magistrates?

GAYMAN   Very well, Sir, and is this your conscience?

SIR CAUTIOUS   Conscience! What do you tell me of conscience? Why, what a noise is here, as if the undoing a young heir were such a wonder! Ods so, I've undone a hundred without half this ado.

GAYMAN   I do believe thee, and am come to tell you I'll be none of that number, for this minute I'll go and redeem it and free myself from the Hell of your indentures.

SIR CAUTIOUS   (How, redeem it! Sure the Devil must help him then.) Stay, Sir, stay. Lord, Sir, what need you put yourself to that trouble? Your land is in safe hands, Sir. Come, come, sit down, and let us take a glass of wine together, Sir.

BELLMOUR   Sir, my service to you.

GAYMAN   Your servant, Sir. (Would I could come to speak to Bellmour, which I dare not do in public, lest I betray him. I long to be resolved where 'twas Sir Feeble was last night — if it were he — by which I might find out my invisible mistress.)

NOISEY   Noble Mr Wasteall.

NOISEY *salutes him, so does* BEARJEST

BELLMOUR   Will you please to sit, Sir?

GAYMAN   I have a little business, Sir, but anon I'll wait on you — your servant, gentlemen — I'll to Crap, the scrivener's.

GAYMAN *goes out*

SIR CAUTIOUS (*to* NOISEY)   Do you know this Wasteall, Sir?

NOISEY   Know him, Sir! Ay, too well.

BEARJEST   The world's well mended with him, Captain, since I lost my money to him and you at the George in Whitefriars.

NOISEY   Ay, poor fellow — he's sometimes up and sometimes down, as the dice favour him.

BEARJEST   Faith and that's pity. But how came he so fine o'th'
sudden? 'Twas but last week he borrowed eighteen pence of me on
his waistbelt to pay his dinner at an ordinary.

BELLMOUR   Were you so cruel, Sir, to take it?

NOISEY   We are not all one man's children. Faith, Sir, we are here
today and gone tomorrow.

SIR CAUTIOUS   I say 'twas done like a wise man, Sir, but under
favour, gentlemen, this Wasteall is a rascal.

NOISEY   A very rascal, Sir, and a most dangerous fellow. He cullies in
your 'prentices and cashiers to play, which ruins so many o'th' young
fry i'th'City.

SIR CAUTIOUS   Hum, does he so, d'ye hear that, Edward?

NOISEY   Then he keeps a private press and prints your Amsterdam
and Leyden libels.

SIR CAUTIOUS   Ay, and makes 'em too, I warrant him. A dangerous
fellow.

NOISEY   Sometimes he begs as a lame soldier with a wooden leg.

BEARJEST   Sometimes, as a blind man, sells switches in Newmarket
Road.

NOISEY   At other times he roams the country like a gypsy; tells
fortunes and robs hedges when he's out of linen.

SIR CAUTIOUS   Tells fortunes, too! Nay, I thought he dealt with the
Devil. Well, gentlemen, you are all wide o' this matter, for to tell you
the truth he deals with the Devil, gentlemen, otherwise he could
never have redeemed his land.

BELLMOUR   How, Sir, the Devil!

SIR CAUTIOUS   I say the Devil! Heaven bless every wise man from
the Devil.

BEARJEST   The Devil, hah! There's no such animal in nature. I rather
think he pads.

NOISEY   Oh Sir, he has not courage for that, but he's an admirable
fellow at your lock.

SIR CAUTIOUS   Lock! My study lock was picked! I begin to suspect
him.

BEARJEST   I saw him once open a lock with the bone of a breast of
mutton, and break an iron bar asunder with the eye of a needle.

SIR CAUTIOUS   Prodigious! Well, I say the Devil still.

Enter SIR FEEBLE

SIR FEEBLE   Who's this talks of the Devil! A pox of the Devil, I say,
this last night's Devil has so haunted me.

SIR CAUTIOUS   Why, have you seen it since, brother?

SIR FEEBLE   In imagination, Sir.

BELLMOUR   How, Sir, a Devil?

SIR FEEBLE   Ay, or a ghost.

BELLMOUR   Where, good Sir?

BEARJEST   Ay, where? I'd travel a hundred mile to see a ghost.

BELLMOUR   Sure, Sir, 'twas fancy.

SIR FEEBLE   If 'twere a fancy, 'twas a strong one; and ghosts and fancy are all one if they can deceive. I tell you, if ever I thought in my life I thought I saw a ghost, ay, and a damnable impudent ghost too, he said he was a fellow here they call Bellmour.

BELLMOUR   How, sir!

BEARJEST   Well, I would give the world to see the Devil, provided he were a civil affable Devil, such a one as Wasteall's acquaintance is.

SIR CAUTIOUS   He can show him too soon, it may be. I'm sure, as civil as he is, he helps him to steal my gold, I doubt, and to be sure, gentlemen, you say he's a gamester. I desire when he comes anon, that you would propose to sport a die or so, and we'll fall to play for a teaster, or the like, and if he sets any money I shall go near to know my own gold, by some remarkable pieces amongst it, and if he have it, I'll hang him, and then his six hundred a year will be my own, which I have in mortgage.

BEARJEST   Let the Captain and I alone to top upon him. Meantime Sir, I have brought my music to entertain my mistress with a song.

SIR FEEBLE   Take your own methods, Sir, they are at leisure, while we go drink their healths within. Adod I long for night. We are not half in kilter, this damned ghost will not out of my head yet.

Exeunt all but BELLMOUR

BELLMOUR   Hah, a ghost! What can he mean? A ghost, and Bellmour's! Sure, my good angel, or my genius, in pity of my love, and of Leticia. But see, Leticia comes, but still attended.

Enter LETICIA, LADY FULBANK, *and* DIANA

BELLMOUR (*aside to her, in passing by*)   (Remember, oh, remember to be true.)

BELLMOUR *goes out*

LADY FULBANK   I was sick to know with what Christian patience you bore the martyrdom of this night.

LETICIA   As those condemned bear the last hour of life. A short reprieve I had, and by a kind mistake, Diana only was my bedfellow. (*She weeps*)

DIANA   I wish for your repose you ne'er had seen my father. (*She too weeps*)

LETICIA   And so do I, I fear he has undone me.

DIANA   And me, in breaking of his word with Bredwell.

LADY FULBANK   So, as Trinculo says, would you were both hanged
    for me, for putting me in mind of my husband, for I have e'en no
    better luck than either of you. Let our two fates warn your approach-
    ing one. I love your Bredwell and must plead for him.
DIANA   I know his virtue justifies my choice, but pride and modesty
    forbids I should, unloved, pursue him.
LETICIA   Wrong not my brother so, who dies for you.
DIANA   Could he so easily see me given away, without a sigh at
    parting? For all the day a calm was in his eyes, and unconcerned he
    looked and talked to me, in dancing never pressed my willing hand,
    nor with a scornful glance reproached my falsehood.
LETICIA   Believe me, that dissembling was his masterpiece.
DIANA   Why should he fear? Did not my father promise him?
LETICIA   Ay, that was in his wooing time to me, but now 'tis all
    forgotten.

Music at the door. After which enter BREDWELL *and* BEARJEST

LADY FULBANK   How now, Cousin! Is this high piece of gallantry
    from you?
BEARJEST   I find my cousin is resolved to conquer. He assails with
    all his artillery of charms. We'll leave him to his success, Madam.

Exeunt LETICIA *and* LADY FULBANK

Oh Lord, Madam, you oblige. Look, Ned, you had a mind to have a
    full view of my mistress, Sir, and here she is. (*He stands gazing*) Go,
    salute her. (Look how he stands now. What a sneaking thing is a
    fellow who has never travelled and seen the world!) Madam, this is
    a very honest friend of mine, for all he looks so simply.
DIANA   Come, he speaks for you, Sir.
BEARJEST   He, Madam! Though he be but a banker's 'prentice, Madam,
    he's as pretty a fellow of his inches as any i'th'City. He has made
    love in dancing schools, and to ladies of quality in the middle gallery,
    and shall joke ye, and repartee with any foreman within the Walls.
    Prithee to her, and commend me. I'll give thee a new point cravat.
DIANA   He looks as if he could not speak to me.
BEARJEST   Not speak to you! Yes, gad Madam, and do anything to
    you too.
DIANA   Are you his advocate, Sir?
BEARJEST (*scornfully*)   For want of a better.

BEARJEST *stands behind* BREDWELL, *pushing him on*

BREDWELL   An advocate for love I am, and bring you such a message
    from a heart.

BEARJEST   Meaning mine, dear Madam.

BREDWELL   That when you hear it, you will pity it.

BEARJEST   (Or the Devil's in her.)

DIANA   I have many reasons to believe it is my fortune you pursue,
not person.

BEARJEST   (There is something in that, I must confess.) But say
what you will, Ned.

BREDWELL   May all the mischiefs of despairing love fall on me if
it be.

BEARJEST   That's well enough.

BREDWELL   No, were you born an humble village maid, that fed a
flock upon the neighbouring plain, with all that shining virtue in
your soul, by Heaven I would adore you, love you, wed you, though
the gay world were lost by such a nuptial;

BEARJEST *looks on him.* BREDWELL *recollects himself*

this I would do, were I my friend the squire.

BEARJEST   Ay, if you were me you might do what you pleased,
but I'm of another mind.

DIANA   Should I consent, my father is a man whom interest sways,
not honour, and whatsoever promises he's made you he means to
break 'em all, and I am destined to another.

BEARJEST   How, another? His name, his name, Madam. Here's Ned
and I fear ne'er a single man i'th'nation. What is he, what is he?

DIANA   A fop, a fool, a beaten ass — a blockhead!

BEARJEST   What a damned shame's this, that women should be
sacrificed to fools, and fops must run away with heiresses, whilst
we men of wit and parts dress and dance, and cock and travel for
nothing but to be tame keepers.

DIANA   But I, by Heaven, will never be that victim.
But where my soul is vowed 'tis fixed forever.

BREDWELL   Are you resolved, are you confirmed in this?
O my Diana, speak it o'er again.

BREDWELL *runs to her, and embraces her*

Bless me, and make me happier than a monarch.

BEARJEST   Hold, hold, dear Ned, that's my part. I take it.

BREDWELL   Your pardon, Sir, I had forgot myself.
But time is short, what's to be done in this?

BEARJEST   Done! I'll enter the house with fire and sword, d'ye see;
not that I care this — but I'll not be fobbed off. What do they take
me for? A fool? An ass?

BREDWELL   Madam, dare you run the risk of your father's displeasure,
and run away with the man you love?

DIANA   With all my soul.

BEARJEST   That's hearty, and we'll do't, Ned and I here. And I love
an amour with an adventure in't, like Amadis de Gaul. Hark ye, Ned,
get a coach and fix ready tonight when 'tis dark at the back gate.

BREDWELL   And I'll get a parson ready in my lodging, to which I
have a key through the garden by which we may pass unseen.

BEARJEST   Good. Mun, here's company.

Enter GAYMAN *with his hat and money in it,* SIR CAUTIOUS *in
a rage,* SIR FEEBLE, LADY FULBANK, LETICIA, CAPTAIN
NOISEY, *and* BELLMOUR

SIR CAUTIOUS   A hundred pound lost already! Oh coxcomb, old
coxcomb, and a wife coxcomb, to turn prodigal at my years. Why,
I was bewitched!

SIR FEEBLE   'Shaw, 'twas a frolic, Sir, I have lost a hundred pound
as well as you. My lady has lost, and your lady has lost, and the rest —
what, old cows will kick sometimes, what's a hundred pound?

SIR CAUTIOUS   A hundred pound! Why 'tis a sum, Sir, a sum!
Why, what the Devil did I do with a box and dice?

LADY FULBANK   Why, you made a shift to lose, Sir! And where's
the harm of that? We have lost and he has won; anon it may be your
fortune.

SIR CAUTIOUS   Ay, but he could never do it fairly, that's certain.
Three hundred pound! Why, how came you to win so unmercifully,
Sir?

GAYMAN   Oh, the Devil will not lose a gamester of me, you see, Sir.

SIR CAUTIOUS   The Devil! Mark that, gentlemen!

BEARJEST   The rogue has damned luck, sure; he has got a fly.

SIR CAUTIOUS   And can you have the conscience to carry away all
our money, Sir?

GAYMAN   Most assuredly, unless you have the courage to retrieve it.
I'll set it at a throw, or any way. What say you gentlemen?

SIR FEEBLE   Ods bobs, you young fellows are too hard for us every
way, and I'm engaged at an old game with a new gamester here who
will require all an old man's stock.

LADY FULBANK   Come Cousin, will you venture a guinea? Come,
Mr Bredwell.

GAYMAN   Well, if nobody dare venture on me, I'll send away my
cash.

They all go to play at the table, leaving SIR CAUTIOUS, SIR FEEBLE
and GAYMAN

SIR CAUTIOUS   Hum, must it all go? (A rare sum, if a man were but
sure the Devil would stand neuter now.) Sir, I wish I had anything
but ready money to stake: three hundred pound, a fine sum!

GAYMAN   You have moveables Sir, goods, commodities.

SIR CAUTIOUS   That's all one, Sir. That's money's worth, Sir, but if
I had anything that were worth nothing.

GAYMAN   You would venture it. I thank you Sir. I would your
lady were worth nothing.

SIR CAUTIOUS   Why so, Sir?

GAYMAN   Then I would set all 'gainst that nothing.

SIR CAUTIOUS   What, set it against my wife?

GAYMAN   Wife, Sir! Ay, your wife.

SIR CAUTIOUS   Hum, my wife against three hundred pounds! What,
all my wife, Sir!

GAYMAN   All your wife! Why Sir, some part of her would serve my
turn.

SIR CAUTIOUS   Hum — my wife. (Why, if I should lose, he could
not have the impudence to take her.)

GAYMAN   Well, I find you are not for the bargain, and so I put up.

SIR CAUTIOUS   Hold, Sir, why so hasty? My wife? No, put up your
money, Sir. What, lose my wife for three hundred pounds!

GAYMAN   Lose her, Sir! Why, she shall be never the worse for my
wearing, Sir! (The old covetous rogue is considering on't I think.)
What say you to a night? I set it to a night. There's none need know
it, Sir.

SIR CAUTIOUS   Hum — a night! Three hundred pounds for a night!
(Why, what a lavish whoremaker's this? We take money to marry
our wives but very seldom part with 'em, and by the bargain get
money.) For a night, say you? (Gad, if I should take the rogue at his
word 'twould be a pure jest.)

SIR FEEBLE   Are you not mad, brother?

SIR CAUTIOUS   No, but I'm wise, and that's as good. Let me
consider.

SIR FEEBLE   What, whether you shall be a cuckold or not?

SIR CAUTIOUS   Or lose three hundred pounds — consider that. A
cuckold! Why 'tis a word, an empty sound; 'tis breath, 'tis air, 'tis
nothing. But three hundred pounds, Lord, what will not three
hundred pounds do? You may chance to be a cuckold for nothing,
Sir.

SIR FEEBLE   It may be so, but she shall do't discreetly then

SIR CAUTIOUS   Under favour, you're an ass, brother. This is the
discreetest way of doing it, I take it.

SIR FEEBLE   But would a wise man expose his wife?

SIR CAUTIOUS   Why, Cato was a wiser man than I, and he lent his
wife to a young fellow they called Hortensius, as story says, and can
a wise man have a better precedent than Cato?

SIR FEEBLE   I say Cato was an ass, Sir, for obliging any young rogue
of 'em all.

SIR CAUTIOUS   But I am of Cato's mind. Well, a single night, you say.

GAYMAN   A single night: to have, to hold, possess and so forth at
discretion.

SIR CAUTIOUS   A night. I shall have her safe and sound i'th'morning?

SIR FEEBLE   Safe, no doubt on't, but how sound?

GAYMAN   And for non-performance you shall pay me three
hundred pounds. I'll forfeit as much if I tell —

SIR CAUTIOUS   Tell? Why, make your three hundred pounds six
hundred, and let it be put into the *Gazette* if you will, man. But is't
a bargain?

GAYMAN   Done. Sir Feeble shall be witness, and there stands my hat.

GAYMAN *puts down his hat of money and each of them takes a box
and dice, and kneel on the stage. The others come and watch*

SIR CAUTIOUS   He that comes first to one and thirty wins.

They throw and count

LADY FULBANK   What are you playing for?

SIR FEEBLE   Nothing, nothing, but a trial of skill between an old
man and a young — and your Ladyship is to be Judge.

LADY FULBANK   I shall be partial, Sir.

SIR CAUTIOUS   Six and five's eleven. (*Throws, and pulls the hat
towards him*)

GAYMAN   Quatre, trois. Pox of the dice.

SIR CAUTIOUS   Two fives — one and twenty. (*Sets up, pulls the hat
nearer*)

GAYMAN   Now, Luck — doublets of sixes — nineteen.

SIR CAUTIOUS   Five and four — thirty. (*Draws the hat to him*)

SIR FEEBLE   Now if he wins it, I'll swear he has a fly indeed. 'Tis
impossible without doublets of sixes.

GAYMAN   Now Fortune smile, and for the future frown. (*Throws*)

SIR CAUTIOUS   Hum, two sixes. (*He rises and looks dolefully around*)

LADY FULBANK   How now? What's the matter you look so like an
ass, what have you lost?

SIR CAUTIOUS   A bauble, a bauble! 'Tis not for what I've lost, but
because I have not won.

SIR FEEBLE   You look very simple, Sir, what think you of Cato now?

SIR CAUTIOUS   A wise man may have his failings.

LADY FULBANK   What has my husband lost?

SIR CAUTIOUS   Only a small parcel of ware that lay dead upon my
hands, sweetheart.

GAYMAN   But I shall improve 'em, Madam, I'll warrant you.

LADY FULBANK   Well, since 'tis no worse, bring in your fine dancer,
Cousin, you say you brought to entertain your mistress with.

BEARJEST *goes out*

GAYMAN   Sir, you'll take care to see me paid tonight?

SIR CAUTIOUS   Well, Sir, but my Lady, you must know, Sir, has
the common frailties of her sex, and will refuse what she even longs
for if persuaded by me.

GAYMAN   'Tis not in my bargain to solicit her, Sir. You are to
procure her, or three hundred pounds, Sir, choose you whether.

SIR CAUTIOUS   Procure her! With all my soul, Sir. Alas, you mistake
my honest meaning, I scorn to be so unjust as not to see you abed
together; and then agree as well as you can, I have done my part. In
order to this, Sir, get but yourself conveyed in a chest to my house
with a direction upon it for me, and for the rest —

GAYMAN   I understand you.

SIR FEEBLE   Ralph, get supper ready.

Enter BEARJEST *with dancers. All go out but* SIR CAUTIOUS

SIR CAUTIOUS   Well, I must break my mind, if possible, to my Lady,
but if she should be refractory now, and make me pay three hundred
pounds. . . ? Why, sure, she won't have so little grace. Three hundred
pounds saved is three hundred pounds got, by our account. Could all
Who of this City-Privilege are free,
Hope to be paid for cuckoldom like me,
Th'unthriving merchant, whom grey hair adorns,
Before all ventures would ensure his horns,
For thus, while he but lets spare rooms to hire,
His wife's cracked credit keeps his own entire.

ACT V

SCENE I

SIR CAUTIOUS' HOUSE

Enter BELLMOUR *alone, sad*

BELLMOUR   The night is come for my Leticia.
The longing bridegroom hastens to his bed,
Whilst she, with all the languishment of love
And sad despair, casts her fair eyes on me,
Which silently implore I would deliver her.
But how. Ay, there's the question — hah —
(*Pausing*)
I'll get myself hid in her bedchamber,
And something I will do may serve us yet.
If all my arts should fail I'll have recourse

(*Draws a dagger*)
To this, and bear Leticia off by force.
But see, she comes.

Enter LADY FULBANK, SIR CAUTIOUS, SIR FEEBLE, LETICIA,
BEARJEST, NOISEY, GAYMAN.   *Exit* BELLMOUR

SIR FEEBLE   Lights there, Ralph. And my Lady's coach there.

BEARJEST *goes to* GAYMAN

BEARJEST   Well, Sir, remember you have promised to grant me my
diabolical request, in showing me the Devil.
GAYMAN   I will not fail you, Sir.
LADY FULBANK   Madam, your servant. I hope you'll see no more
ghosts, Sir Feeble.
SIR FEEBLE   No more of that, I beseech you, Madam. Prithee, Sir
Cautious, take away your wife. Madam, your servant.

They all go out after the light.

Come, Lette, Lette, hasten, rogue, hasten to thy chamber; away, here
be the young wenches coming.

Puts her out, he goes out

Enter DIANA, *puts on her hood and scarf*

DIANA   So, they are gone to bed. And now for Bredwell.
The coach waits and I'll take this opportunity.
Father, farewell. If you dislike my course,
Blame the old rigid customs of your force.

She goes out

SCENE II

A BEDCHAMBER

Enter SIR FEEBLE, LETICIA *and* PHILLIS

LETICIA   Ah, Phillis! I am fainting with my fears. Hast thou no
comfort for me?

SIR FEEBLE *undresses to his gown*

SIR FEEBLE   Why, what art doing there, fiddle fadling? Adod, you
young wenches are so loth to come to but when your hand's in. You
have no mercy upon us poor husbands.
LETICIA   Why do you talk so, Sir?
SIR FEEBLE   Was it angered at the Fool's prattle? tum-a-me, tum-a-me,

I'll undress it, effags I will, roguey.

LETICIA   You are so wanton, Sir, you make me blush. I will not go
to bed unless you'll promise me.

SIR FEEBLE   No bargaining, my little hussy. What, you'll tie my
hands behind me, will you?

She goes to the table

LETICIA   What shall I do? Assist me, gentle maid, thy eyes methinks
put on a little hope.

PHILLIS   Take courage, Madam, you guess right. Be confident.

SIR FEEBLE   No whispering, gentlewoman, and putting tricks into
her head that shall cheat me of another night. Look on that silly
little round chitty-face, look on those smiling roguish loving eyes
there, look, look how they laugh, twire and tempt. He, rogue, I'll
buss 'em there, and here, and everywhere. Ods bobs, away, this is
fooling and spoiling of a man's stomach, with a bit here and a bit
there. To bed, to bed.

*As she is sitting at her dressing table, he looks over her shoulder, and
sees her face in the glass*

LETICIA   Go you first, Sir, I will but stay to say my prayers (which
are that Heaven would deliver me).

SIR FEEBLE   Say thy prayers! What, art thou mad! Prayers upon
thy wedding night! A short thanksgiving or so, but prayers, quoth
'a. . . 'Sbobs you'll have time enough for that, I doubt.

LETICIA   I am ashamed to undress before you, Sir. Go to bed.

SIR FEEBLE   What, was it ashamed to show its little white foots, and
its little round bubbies? Well, I'll go, I'll go. I cannot think on't, no,
I cannot.

Going towards the bed, BELLMOUR *comes forth from between the
curtains, his coat off, his shirt bloody, a dagger in his hand, and his
disguise off*

BELLMOUR   Stand!

SIR FEEBLE   Ah!

LETICIA
and PHILLIS } (*squeak*)   Oh, Heavens!

LETICIA   Why, is it Bellmour?

BELLMOUR   Go not to bed! I guard this sacred place, and the
adulterer dies that enters here.

SIR FEEBLE   (Oh, why do I shake?) Sure I'm a man, what are thou?

BELLMOUR   I am the wronged, the lost and murdered Bellmour.

SIR FEEBLE   Oh, Lord, it is the same I saw last night — Oh! Hold thy
dread vengeance, pity me, and hear me. Oh! a pardon, a pardon.
(What shall I do? Oh! where shall I hide myself?)

BELLMOUR   I'th'utmost borders of the earth I'll find thee.
Seas shall not hide thee, nor vast mountains guard thee.
Even in the depth of Hell I'll find thee out,
And lash thy filthy and adulterous soul.

SIR FEEBLE   Oh, I am dead, I'm dead! Will no repentance save me?
'Twas that young Eve that tempted me to sin. Oh!

BELLMOUR   See, fair seducer, what thou'st made me do;
Look on this bleeding wound, it reached my heart,
To pluck my dear tormenting image thence,
When news arrived that thou had'st broke thy vow.

LETICIA   Oh hide that fatal wound, my tender heart faints with a
sight so horrid! (*She seems to weep*)

SIR FEEBLE   So, she'll clear herself, and leave me in the Devil's
clutches.

BELLMOUR   You've both offended Heaven, and must repent or die.

SIR FEEBLE   Ah, I do confess I was an old fool, bewitched with
beauty, besotted with love, and do repent most heartily.

BELLMOUR   No, you had rather yet go on in sin.
Thou wouldst live on, and be a baffled cuckold.

SIR FEEBLE   Oh, not for the world, Sir! I am convinced and mortified.

BELLMOUR   Maintain her fine, undo thy peace to please her, and still
be cuckold'on, believe her, trust her and be cuckolded still.

SIR FEEBLE   I see my folly, and my age's dotage, and find the Devil
was in me. Yet spare my age, ah, spare me to repent.

BELLMOUR   If thou repent'st, renounce her, fly her sight,
Shun her bewitching charms, as thou would'st Hell,
Those dark eternal mansions of the dead
Whither I must descend.

SIR FEEBLE   Oh, would he were gone!

BELLMOUR   Fly, be gone, depart, vanish forever from her to some
more safe and innocent apartment.

SIR FEEBLE   Oh, that's very hard.

He goes back trembling, BELLMOUR *follows in, with his dagger up,
both go out*

LETICIA   Blest be this kind release, and yet, methinks, it grieves me
to consider how the poor old man is frighted.

BELLMOUR *re-enters, puts on his coat*

BELLMOUR   He's gone, and locked himself into his chamber, and
now, my dear Leticia, let us fly.
Despair till now did my wild heart invade,
But pitying love has the rough storm allayed.

Exeunt

SCENE III

SIR CAUTIOUS FULBANK'S GARDEN

Enter two PORTERS *and* RAG, *bearing* GAYMAN *in a chest. They set it down. He comes forth with a dark lantern*

GAYMAN   Set down the chest behind yon hedge of roses, and then put on those shapes I have appointed you, and be sure you well-favouredly bang both Bearjest and Noisey, since they have a mind to see the Devil.

RAG   Oh, Sir, leave 'em to us for that, and if we do not play the Devil with 'em, we deserve they should beat us. But Sir, we are in Sir Cautious' garden, will he not sue us for a trespass?

GAYMAN   I'll bear you out, be ready at my call.

They all go out, leaving GAYMAN

Let me see. I have got no ready stuff to banter with, but no matter, any gibberish will serve the fools. 'Tis now about the hour of ten, but twelve is my appointed lucky minute, when all the blessings that my soul could wish shall be resigned to me.

Enter BREDWELL

Hah! Who's there? Bredwell?

BREDWELL   Oh, are you come, Sir, and can you be so kind to a poor youth, to favour his designs and bless his days?

GAYMAN   Yes, I am ready here with all my Devils, both to secure you your mistress, and to cudgel your Captain and Squire for abusing me behind my back so basely.

BREDWELL   'Twas most unmanly, Sir, and they deserve it. I wonder that they come not.

GAYMAN   How durst you trust her with him?

BREDWELL   Because 'tis dangerous to steal a City heiress. And let the theft be his, so the dear maid be mine. Hark — sure they come.

Enter BEARJEST, *who runs into* BREDWELL

Who's there, Mr Bearjest?

BEARJEST   Who's that, Ned? Well, I have brought my mistress. Hast thou got a parson ready, and a licence?

BREDWELL   Ay, ay, but where's the lady?

BEARJEST   In the coach, with the Captain, at the gate. I came before to see if the coast be clear.

BREDWELL   Ay, Sir, but what shall we do? Here's Mr Gayman come on purpose to show you the Devil as you desired.

BEARJEST   Pshaw! A pox of the Devil, man, I can't attend to speak with him now.

GAYMAN   How, Sir! Do you think my Devil of so little quality to suffer an affront unrevenged?

BEARJEST   Sir, I cry his Devilship's pardon, I did not know his quality. I protest Sir, I love and honour him, but I am now just going to be married, Sir, and when that ceremony's past I'm ready to go to the Devil as soon as you please.

GAYMAN   I have told him your desire of seeing him and should you baffle him?

BEARJEST   Who I, Sir? Pray let his Worship know I shall be proud of the honour of his acquaintance, but, Sir, my mistress and the parson wait in Ned's chamber.

GAYMAN   If all the world wait, Sir, the Prince of Hell will stay for no man.

BREDWELL   Oh Sir, rather than the Prince of the Infernals shall be affronted, I'll conduct the lady up, and entertain her till you come Sir.

BEARJEST   Nay, I have a great mind to kiss his paw, Sir, but I could wish you'd show him me by daylight, Sir.

GAYMAN   The Prince of Darkness does abhor the light. But, Sir, I will for once allow your friend the Captain to keep you company.

Enter NOISEY *and* DIANA

BEARJEST   I'm much obliged to you, Sir. Oh, Captain — (*Talks to him*)

BREDWELL   Haste dear, the parson waits,
To finish what the Powers designed above.

DIANA   Sure, nothing is so bold as maids in love.

They go out

NOISEY   Pshaw! He, conjure? He can fly as soon.

GAYMAN   Gentlemen, you must be sure to confine yourselves to this circle, and have a care you neither swear, nor pray.

BEARJEST   Pray, Sir! I dare say neither of us were ever that way gifted.

A horrid noise, then soft music

GAYMAN·   Cease your horror, cease your haste,
And calmly as I saw you last,
Appear! Appear!
By the pearls and diamond rocks,
By thy heavy money-box,
By thy shining petticoat,
That hid thy cloven feet from note,
By the veil that hid thy face,
Which else had fright'd human race,

Appear, that I thy love may see,
Appear, kind fiends, appear to me.

Soft music ceases

(A pox of these rascals, why come they not?)

Four enter from the four corners of the stage. To music that plays they dance, and in the dance, dance around BEARJEST *and* NOISEY *and kick, pinch and beat them*

BEARJEST   Oh, enough, enough! Good Sir, lay 'em, and I'll pay the music.

GAYMAN   I wonder at it. These spirits are in their nature kind and peaceable, but you have basely injured somebody; confess and they will be satisfied.

BEARJEST   Oh good Sir, take you your Cerberuses off. I do confess, the Captain here and I have violated your fame.

NOISEY   Abused you and traduced you, and thus we beg your pardon.

GAYMAN   Abused me! 'Tis more than I know, gentlemen.

BEARJEST   But it seems your friend the Devil does.

GAYMAN   (By this time Bredwell's married.) Great Pantamogun, hold, for I am satisfied.

Exeunt DEVILS

And thus undo my charm.

Takes away the circle. BEARJEST *and* NOISEY *run out*

So, the fools are gone. And now to Julia's arms.

SCENE IV

LADY FULBANK'S ANTE-CHAMBER

She is discovered at her glass with SIR CAUTIOUS, *undressed*

LADY FULBANK   But why tonight? Indeed you're wondrous kind, methinks.

SIR CAUTIOUS   Why, I don't know, a wedding is a sort of an alarm to love, it calls up every man's courage.

LADY FULBANK   Ay, but will it come when 'tis called?

SIR CAUTIOUS   (I doubt you'll find it, to my grief.) But I think 'tis all one to thee, thou care'st not for my compliment, no, thou'dst rather have a young fellow.

LADY FULBANK   I am not used to flatter much. If forty years were taken from your age 'twould render you something more agreeable to my bed, I must confess.

SIR CAUTIOUS   Ay, ay, no doubt on't.

LADY FULBANK   Yet you may take my word without an oath; were
you as old as Time and I were young and gay as April flowers, which
all are fond to gather, my beauties all should wither in the shade, e'er
I'd be worn in a dishonest bosom.

SIR CAUTIOUS   Ay, but you're wondrous free methinks, sometimes,
which gives shrewd suspicions.

LADY FULBANK   What, because I cannot simper, look demure, and
justify my honour when none questions it? Cry 'fie', and 'out
upon the naughty women', because they please themselves, and so
would I?

SIR CAUTIOUS   How, would what, cuckold me?

LADY FULBANK   Yes, if it pleased me better than virtue, Sir. But
I'll not change my freedom and my humour, to purchase the dull
fame of being honest.

SIR CAUTIOUS   Ay, but the world, the world.

LADY FULBANK   I value not the censures of the crowd.

SIR CAUTIOUS   But I am old.

LADY FULBANK   That's your fault, not mine.

SIR CAUTIOUS   But being so, if I should be good-natured and give
thee leave to love discreetly —

LADY FULBANK   I'd do't without your leave, Sir.

SIR CAUTIOUS   Do't? What, cuckold me!

LADY FULBANK   No, love discreetly, Sir, love as I ought, love
honestly.

SIR CAUTIOUS   What, in love with anybody but your own husband?

LADY FULBANK   Yes.

SIR CAUTIOUS   Yes, quoth'a! Is that your loving as you ought?

LADY FULBANK   We cannot help our inclinations, Sir, no more than
time or light from coming on. But I can keep my virtue, Sir, entire.

SIR CAUTIOUS   What, I'll warrant, this is your first love, Gayman?

LADY FULBANK   I'll not deny that truth, though even to you.

SIR CAUTIOUS   Why, in consideration of my age, and your youth,
I'd bear a conscience provided you do things wisely.

LADY FULBANK   Do what thing, Sir?

SIR CAUTIOUS   You know what I mean. . .

LADY FULBANK   Hah — I hope you would not be a cuckold, Sir.

SIR CAUTIOUS   Why, truly in a civil way, or so.

LADY FULBANK   There is but one way, Sir, to make me hate you,
and that would be tame suffering.

SIR CAUTIOUS   (Nay, and she be thereabouts there's no discovering.)

LADY FULBANK   But leave this fond discourse, and, if you must, let
us to bed.

SIR CAUTIOUS   Ay, ay, I did but try your virtue, mun, dost think
I was in earnest?

Enter SERVANT

SERVANT   Sir, here's a chest directed to your Worship.
SIR CAUTIOUS   (Hum, 'tis Wasteall. Now does my heart fail me.)
A chest, say you. . . to me. . . so late. I'll warrant it comes from
Sir Nicholas Smuggle, some prohibited goods that he has stolen the
custom of and cheated his Majesty. Well, he's an honest man, bring
it in.

Exit SERVANT

LADY FULBANK   What, into my apartment, Sir, a nasty chest?
SIR CAUTIOUS   By all means, for if the searchers come, they'll never
be so uncivil to ransack thy lodgings, and we are bound in Christian
charity to do for one another. Some rich commodities, I am sure, and
some fine nic-nac will fall to thy share, I'll warrant thee. (Pox on him
for a young rogue, how punctual he is!)

SERVANTS *re-enter with the chest*

Go, my dear, go to bed. I'll send Sir Nicholas a receipt for the chest,
and be with thee presently.

SIR CAUTIOUS, SERVANTS *and* LADY FULBANK *leave*

GAYMAN *peeps out of the chest, and looks round him, wondering*

GAYMAN   Hah, where am I? By Heaven, my last night's vision! 'Tis
that enchanted room, and yonder's the alcove! Sure 'twas indeed
some witch, who, knowing of my infidelity, has by enchantment
brought me hither. 'Tis so, I am betrayed. (*He pauses*) Hah! Or was
it Julia that last night gave me that lone opportunity? But hark, I
hear someone coming. (*He shuts himself in*)

Enter SIR CAUTIOUS

SIR CAUTIOUS (*lifting up the chest-lid*)   So, you are come, I see. (*He
goes and locks the door*)
GAYMAN   (Hah — he here! Nay then, I was deceived, and it was
Julia that last night gave me the dear assignation.)

SIR CAUTIOUS *peeps into the main bedchamber*

LADY FULBANK (*within*)   Come, Sir Cautious, I shall fall asleep
and then you'll waken me.
SIR CAUTIOUS   Ay, my dear, I'm coming. She's in bed. I'll go put
out the candle and then. . .
GAYMAN   Ay, I'll warrant you for my part.
SIR CAUTIOUS   Ay, but you may over-act your part, and spoil all.
But, Sir, I hope you'll use a Christian conscience in this business.

GAYMAN   Oh doubt not, Sir, but I shall do you reason.

SIR CAUTIOUS   Ay, Sir, but. . .

GAYMAN   Good Sir, no more cautions; you, unlike a fair gamester, will rook me out of half my night. I am impatient.

SIR CAUTIOUS   Good Lord, are you so hasty? If I please, you shan't go at all.

GAYMAN   With all my soul, Sir. Pay me three hundred pounds, Sir.

SIR CAUTIOUS   Lord, Sir, you mistake my candid meaning still. I am content to be a cuckold, Sir, but I would have things done decently, d'ye mind me?

GAYMAN   As decently as a cuckold can be made, Sir. But no more disputes, I pray, Sir.

SIR CAUTIOUS   I'm gone! I'm gone! But hark ye, Sir, you'll rise before day?

SIR CAUTIOUS goes out, then returns

GAYMAN   Yet again!

SIR CAUTIOUS   I vanish, Sir, but hark ye, you'll not speak a word, but let her think 'tis I.

GAYMAN   Begone, I say, Sir.

SIR CAUTIOUS runs out

I am convinced last night I was with Julia.
O sot, insensible and dull!

Enter softly to the main bedchamber SIR CAUTIOUS

SIR CAUTIOUS   So, the candle's out. Give me your hand.

He leads GAYMAN softly in

SCENE V

SCENE CHANGES TO THE BEDCHAMBER

LADY FULBANK *supposed in bed.*
Enter SIR CAUTIOUS and GAYMAN by dark

SIR CAUTIOUS   Where are you, my dear? (*He leads GAYMAN to the bed*)

LADY FULBANK   Where should I be? In bed. What, are you by dark?

SIR CAUTIOUS   Ay, the candle went out by chance.

GAYMAN signs to him to be gone. He makes grimaces as loth to go, and exits

SCENE VI

SCENE DRAWS OVER, AND REPRESENTS ANOTHER ROOM
IN THE SAME HOUSE

Enter PARSON, DIANA *and* PERT *dressed in* DIANA's *clothes*

DIANA   I'll swear, Mrs Pert, you look very prettily in my clothes,
and since you, Sir, have convinced me that this innocent deceit is not
unlawful, I am glad to be the instrument of advancing Mrs Pert to a
husband she already has so just a claim to.
PARSON   Since she has so firm a contract, I pronounce it a lawful
marriage. But hark, they are coming, sure.
DIANA   Pull your hoods down, and keep your face from the light.

DIANA *runs out*

Enter BEARJEST *and* NOISEY, *disordered*

BEARJEST   Madam, I beg your pardon. I met with a most devilish
adventure. Your pardon too, Mr Doctor, for making you wait. But
the business is this, Sir, I have a great mind to lie with this young
gentlewoman tonight, but she swears if I do the parson of the parish
shall know it.
PARSON   If I do, Sir, I shall keep counsel.
BEARJEST   And that's civil, Sir. Come, lead the way,
With such a guide, the Devil's in't if we can go astray.

SCENE VII

SCENE CHANGES TO THE ANTE-CHAMBER

Enter SIR CAUTIOUS

SIR CAUTIOUS   Now cannot I sleep, but am as restless as a merchant
in stormy weather, that has ventured all his wealth in one bottom.
Woman is a leaky vessel: if she should like the young rogue now, and
they should come to a right understanding, why then I am a Wittal,
that's all, and shall be put in print at Snowhill with my effigies
o'th'top, like the sign of Cuckold's Haven. Hum, they're damnable
silent. Pray Heaven he has not murdered her, and robbed her. Hum,
hark, what's that? A noise! He has broke his covenant with me, and
shall forfeit the money. How loud they are! Ay, ay, the plot's
discovered, what shall I do? Why, the Devil is not in her, sure, to be
refractory now, and peevish. If she be, I must pay my money yet,

and that would be a damned thing. Sure, they're coming out. I'll
retire and hear how 'tis with them.

He retires

Enter LADY FULBANK *undressed,* GAYMAN *half undressed upon
his knees following her, holding her gown*

LADY FULBANK   Oh! You unkind! What have you made me do?
Unhand me, false deceiver, let me loose!
SIR CAUTIOUS (*peeping*)   Made her do? So, so, 'tis done. I'm glad
of that.
GAYMAN   Can you be angry, Julia, because I only seized my right of
love.
LADY FULBANK   And must my honour be the price of it? Could
nothing but my fame reward your passion? What, make me a base
prostitute, a foul adult'ress? Oh, be gone, be gone, dear robber of my
quiet.
SIR CAUTIOUS   (Oh fearful!)
GAYMAN   Oh! Calm your rage, and hear me. If you are so,
You are an innocent adult'ress.
It was the feeble husband you enjoyed
In cold imagination, and no more.
Shyly you turned away, faintly resigned.
SIR CAUTIOUS   (Hum, did she so?)
GAYMAN   Till excess of love betrayed the cheat.
SIR CAUTIOUS   (Ay, ay, that was my fear.)
LADY FULBANK   Away, be gone. I'll never see you more.
GAYMAN   You may as well forbid the Sun to shine.
Not see you more! Heavens! I before adored you,
But now I rave! And with my impatient love,
A thousand mad and wild desires are burning!
I have discovered now new worlds of charms,
And can no longer tamely love and suffer.
SIR CAUTIOUS   (So, I have brought an old house upon my head,
Entailed cuckoldom upon myself.)
LADY FULBANK   I'll hear no more. Sir Cautious! Where's my
husband? Why have you left my honour thus unguarded?
SIR CAUTIOUS   (Ay, ay, she's well enough pleased, I fear, for all.)
GAYMAN   Base as he is, 'twas he exposed this treasure, like silly
Indians bartered thee for trifles.
SIR CAUTIOUS   (Oh treacherous villain!)
LADY FULBANK   Hah, my husband do this?
GAYMAN   He, by love, he was the kind procurer,
Contrived the means, and brought me to thy bed.
LADY FULBANK   My husband! My wise husband!

What fondness in my conduct had he seen,
To take so shameful and so base revenge?

GAYMAN   None. 'Twas filthy avarice seduced him to't.

LADY FULBANK   If he could be so barbarous to expose me,
Could you, who loved me, be so cruel too?

GAYMAN   What, to possess thee when the bliss was offered?
Possess thee too without a crime to thee?
Charge not my soul with so remiss a flame,
So dull a sense of virtue to refuse it.

LADY FULBANK   I am convinced the fault was all my husband's.
(*Kneels*) And here I vow, by all things just and sacred,
To separate forever from his bed.

SIR CAUTIOUS   (Oh, I am not able to endure it.)
Hold, oh hold, my dear.

He kneels as she rises

LADY FULBANK   Stand off! I do abhor thee.

SIR CAUTIOUS   With all my soul, but do not make rash vows, they
break my very heart. Regard my reputation.

LADY FULBANK   Which you have had such care of, Sir, already.
Rise, 'tis in vain you kneel.

SIR CAUTIOUS   No, I'll never rise again. Alas! Madam, I was merely
drawn in. I only thought to sport a die or so, I had only an innocent
design to have discovered whether this gentleman had stolen my gold,
that so I might have hanged him.

GAYMAN   A very innocent design, indeed!

SIR CAUTIOUS   Ay, Sir, that's all, as I'm an honest man.

LADY FULBANK   I've sworn, nor are the stars more fixed than I.

Enter SERVANT

SERVANT   How! my Lady, and his Worship up? Madam, a gentleman
and a lady below in a coach knocked me up, and say they must speak
with your Ladyship.

LADY FULBANK   This is strange! Bring them up.

Exit SERVANT

Who can it be, at this odd time of neither night nor day?

Enter LETICIA, BELLMOUR *and* PHILLIS

LETICIA   Madam, your virtue, charity and friendship to me, has made
me trespass on you for my life's security, and beg you will protect
me, and my husband.

She points at BELLMOUR

SIR CAUTIOUS   So, here's another sad catastrophe!

LADY FULBANK   Hah, does Bellmour live? Is't possible? Believe me, Sir, you ever had my wishes, and shall not fail of my protection now.

BELLMOUR   I humbly thank your Ladyship.

GAYMAN   I'm glad thou hast her, Harry, but doubt thou durst not own her. Nay, durst not own thyself.

BELLMOUR   Yes, friend, I have my pardon.
But, hark, I think we are pursued already;
But now I fear no force.

A noise of somebody coming in

LADY FULBANK   However, step into my bedchamber.

Exeunt LETICIA, GAYMAN, BELLMOUR *and* PHILLIS

Enter SIR FEEBLE *in an antic manner*

SIR FEEBLE   Hell shall not hold thee, nor vast mountains cover thee, but I will find thee out and lash thy filthy and adulterous carcass.

Coming up in a menacing manner to SIR CAUTIOUS

SIR CAUTIOUS   How, lash my filthy carcass? I defy thee, Satan.

SIR FEEBLE   'Twas thus he said.

SIR CAUTIOUS   Let who will say it, he lies in's throat.

SIR FEEBLE   How, the ghostly, hush, have a care, for 'twas the ghost of Bellmour. Oh, hide that bleeding wound, it chills my soul!

Runs to LADY FULBANK

LADY FULBANK   What bleeding wound? Heavens, are you frantic, Sir?

SIR FEEBLE   No. But for want of rest, I shall e'er morning. She's gone, she's gone, she's gone. (*He weeps*)

SIR CAUTIOUS   Ay, ay, she's gone, she's gone, indeed. (*He weeps too*)

SIR FEEBLE   But her let go, so I may never see that dreaded vision. . .
Hark ye, Sir, a word in your ear: have a care of marrying a young wife.

SIR CAUTIOUS (*weeping*)   Ay, but I have married one already.

SIR FEEBLE   Hast thou? Divorce her, fly her, quick. Depart, be gone, she'll cuckold thee, and still she'll cuckold thee.

SIR CAUTIOUS   Ay, brother, but whose fault was that? Why, are not you married?

SIR FEEBLE   Mum! No words on't, unless you'll have the ghost about your ears. Part with your wife, I say, or else the Devil will part ye.

LADY FULBANK   Pray go to bed, Sir.

SIR FEEBLE   Yes, for I shall sleep now I shall lie alone. (*Weeps*)
Ah, fool, old, dull, besotted fool, to think she'd love me. 'Twas

by base means I gained her; cozened an honest gentleman of fame
and life.

LADY FULBANK   You did so, Sir, but 'tis not past redress, you may
make that honest gentleman amends.

SIR FEEBLE   Oh would I could, so I gave half my estate.

LADY FULBANK   That penitence atones with him and Heaven.
Come forth, Leticia, and your injured ghost.

Re-enter LETICIA, GAYMAN, BELLMOUR *and* PHILLIS

SIR FEEBLE   Hah, ghost! Another sight would make me mad indeed.

BELLMOUR   Behold me, Sir, I have no terror now.

SIR FEEBLE   Hah, who's that, Francis! My nephew Francis?

BELLMOUR   Bellmour, or Francis, choose you which you like, and I
am either.

SIR FEEBLE   Hah, Bellmour! And no ghost?

BELLMOUR   Bellmour, and not your nephew, Sir.

SIR FEEBLE   But art alive? Ods bobs, I'm glad on't, Sirrah. But are
you the real Bellmour?

BELLMOUR   As sure as I'm no ghost.

GAYMAN   We all can witness for him, Sir.

SIR FEEBLE   Where be the minstrels? We'll have a dance, adod we
will. Ah! Art thou there, thou cozening little chits-face? A vengeance
on thee, thou madest me an old, doting, loving coxcomb, but I forgive
thee, and give thee all thy jewels, and you your pardon, Sir, so you'll
give me mine, for I find you young knaves will be too hard for us.

BELLMOUR   You are so generous, Sir, that 'tis almost with grief I
receive the blessing of Leticia.

SIR FEEBLE   No, no, thou deservest her, she would have made an
old, fond blockhead of me, and one way or other you would have
had her, ods bobs, you would.

Enter BEARJEST, DIANA, PERT, BREDWELL *and* NOISEY

BEARJEST   Justice, Sir, justice! I have been cheated, abused,
assassinated and ravished!

SIR CAUTIOUS   How, my nephew ravished?

PERT   No, Sir, I am his wife.

SIR CAUTIOUS   Hum! My heir marry a chambermaid!

BEARJEST   Sir, you must know I stole away Mrs Dy, and brought her
to Ned's chamber here to marry her.

SIR FEEBLE   My daughter Dy stolen!

BEARJEST   But I being to go to the Devil a little, Sir, whip, what
does he, but marries her himself, Sir, and fobbed me off here with my
lady's cast petticoat.

NOISEY   Sir, she's a gentlewoman, and my sister, Sir.

PERT   Madam, 'twas a pious fraud, if it were one, for I was contracted
to him before. See, here it is.

Gives it 'em

ALL   A plain case, a plain case.

SIR FEEBLE   Hark ye, Sir, have you had the impudence to marry my daughter, Sir?

To BREDWELL, *who, with* DIANA, *kneels*

BREDWELL   Yes, Sir, and humbly ask your pardon, and your blessing.

SIR FEEBLE   You will ha't, whether I will or not, rise, you are still too hard for us. Come, Sir, forgive your nephew.

SIR CAUTIOUS   Well, Sir, I will, but all this while you little think the tribulation I am in; my Lady has forsworn my bed.

SIR FEEBLE   Indeed, Sir, the wiser she.

SIR CAUTIOUS   For only performing my promise to this gentleman.

SIR FEEBLE   Ay, you showed her the difference, Sir, you're a wise man. Come, dry your eyes, and rest yourself contented. We are a couple of old coxcombs. D'ye hear, Sir, coxcombs.

SIR CAUTIOUS   I grant it, Sir, and if I die, Sir, I bequeath my Lady to you, with my whole estate. My nephew has too much already for a fool. (*To* GAYMAN)

GAYMAN   I thank you, Sir. Do you consent, my Julia?

LADY FULBANK   No, Sir, you do not like me: 'a canvas bag of wooden ladles were a better bedfellow'.

GAYMAN   Cruel tormentor! Oh, I could kill myself with shame and anger!

LADY FULBANK   Come hither, Bredwell. Witness for my honour, that I had no design upon his person but that of trying his constancy.

BREDWELL   Believe me, Sir, 'tis true I feigned a danger near just as you got to bed, and I was the kind Devil, Sir, that brought the gold to you.

BEARJEST   And you were one of the Devils that beat me and the Captain here, Sir?

GAYMAN   No, truly, Sir, those were some I hired to beat you for abusing me today.

NOISEY   To make you amends, Sir, I bring you the certain news of the death of Sir Thomas Gayman, your uncle, who has left you two thousand pounds a year.

GAYMAN   I thank you, Sir. I heard the news before.

SIR CAUTIOUS   How's this, Mr Gayman, my Lady's first lover?
I find, Sir Feeble, we were a couple of old fools indeed, to think at our age to cozen two lusty young fellows of their mistresses. 'Tis no wonder that both the men and the women have been too hard for us; we are not fit matches for either, that's the truth on't.
That warrior needs must to his rival yield,
Who comes with blunted weapons to the field.

Appendix

The following Prologue was used in the WPT's production of *The Lucky Chance*.

Prologue

A dance.

SIR CAUTIOUS: Sir Cautious Fulbank. Married to Julia.

JULIA: Julia. Married to Sir Cautious. In love with Gayman.

GAYMAN: Gayman. Destitute. In love with Julia.

SIR FEEBLE: Sir Feeble Fainwood. About to marry Leticia.

LETICIA: Leticia. Soon to marry Sir Feeble. In love with Bellmour.

BELLMOUR: Bellmour. Banished. In love with Leticia.

BEARJEST: Bearjest. Betrothed to Diana.

DIANA: Diana. Betrothed to Bearjest. In love with Bredwell.

BREDWELL: Bredwell. Leticia's brother. In love with Diana.

PAM FERRIS: Fiddler. Gingle. Phillis. Ralph. Postman. Pert. Captain Noisey. Rag. Landlady and Dick.